My Life
NO BULL

My Life

NO BULL

MIKE ASHCROFT

Paperback: 978-1-959082-40-8
eBook: 978-1-959082-41-5
Library of Congress Control Number: 2022915770

Ordering Information:

BookTrail Agency
8838 Sleepy Hollow Rd.
Kansas City, MO 64114

Printed in the United States of America

CONTENTS

PREFACE

I HOPE YOU WILL learn through reading this that my decision making skills sometimes need a bit of help, but, that it all works out fine in the end.

I feel I have been tremendously lucky and privileged to have had the lives (yes, it does feel like more than one) I've had.

The people who have had walk-on or more starring rôles in my story have helped shape me into the Buddha lookalike I've grown into.

People often say that when you come from a "broken" home life will be harder for you.

My home, and my life have never felt "broken", far from it. As opportunities and experiences have presented themselves, pretty much I've jumped in with both feet.

So, whether you were a walk-on or a major player, or, even if you didn't get a mention by name, thank you.

It's been a rollercoaster and an absolute JOY.

Rare photo of all 4 brothers

CHAPTER 1
PRECONCEPTION TO PRESCHOOL

My Mother is German. She is, as I write this, 94 years old and still lives in Kaarst near Düsseldorf in Germany. She met my Father after the war as a translator in the British Consulate. The only part he had in my life was helping create me, and my three brothers. Other than that he was a vile bullying philandering piece of garbage. He gets no more of this story.

My older brother Peter was born in Germany. I always believed I was conceived in England, but only with the Queens Platinum Jubilee did my Mother describe her first day in England.

She thought it strange that so many shops displayed purple fabric and a picture of the King.

It was the day he died. February 1952, I was born on 23rd June 1952 so was actually conceived in Germany.

Apparently the "flat" that my Father had rented had a lot of women going in and out of the other flats day and night. He'd moved My Mother and older brother into a brothel.

They moved to a house in Merstham in Surrey before I arrived.

As my Mothers second child, the midwives at Redhill Hospital were impatient with my Mothers insistence that I was imminent, telling her she should know better. She did know better.

Having almost been born in the lift, I slipped quietly into the World after only 2 hours of labour. Much to the annoyance of another lady on the ward who complained loudly about how unfair it was as she had been there 36 hours.

My Father wanted to call me Robert Sidney.

Thankfully my Mother had other ideas, and got to the Registry Office first. There I was. Michael Charles Ashcroft. No doubt the most gorgeous baby in the hospital.

I've always had a problem with hiding my modesty and shyness.

Obviously, all this part isn't from my own memory, we were all extremely lucky to get our Mother as ours.

She has lived her whole life fighting like a lioness to protect her sons, often from their pig of a father.

Unbeknown to me obviously, he was putting himself about on a regular basis with random women. He was careless with his fists and would regularly beat my Mother up.

But, as most women did in those days, she stayed for her children.

4 years later my brother Andrew (Andy) came along, the full set being completed by my "baby brother" (he will always be that to me), Mark, in 1960 So let's go back a bit to my earliest memories.

Our German Grandparents Omi and Opi, idolised us, as we did them.

Opi was a bit of a drinker, which, having heard about his history was none too surprising.

He was a Conscientious Objector in WW1. As a result they got the most dangerous jobs of all. Stretcher bearers into No Mans Land under heavy fire rescuing whom they could. He was eventually (many years after WW1) awarded a bravery medal which my Grandmother had to sell to get food when there was none.

In WW2 he was in the German equivalent of the Home Guard and was also attached to an Anti-aircraft battery.

They lived in Wuppertal, a small city in the Ruhr. Famous for the suspended monorail, the Schwebebahn (still there) and being the HQ of Bayer, the chemical company. This was a major target for the RAF in the War, and hence, the town was heavily bombed.

My Grandmother Omi, was a short fat woman with thin arms and legs, and, despite loving her dearly, we called her Sputnik (Google it). Her mission in life was to get as many calories into us as we could take.

These days we would call her a feeder, then, we called her Omi.

Her baking was particularly appealing to me, I've never been short of a calorie to this day.

We travelled to visit them fairly regularly. I can still remember the terror on the train each time we stopped at places like Brussels, when our Mother would get off to buy sandwiches etc. we thought we'd never see her again.

On one of our stays, aged about 3 or 4, with them I caught scarlet fever, and had to be left behind when my Mother and brother returned home. As it turned out this was an important event in several ways. In my 3 months with them I forgot how to speak English (they spoke virtually none). This explains why I am fluent in German, more about that later.

It also explains one of my phobias. The fear of heights.

They lived on the second floor of a block of large elegant flats in Wuppertal. It had almost floor to (high) ceiling windows.

Apparently I was very fond of the horse that pulled the milkman's cart. He (the milkman, not the horse) would announce his presence by ringing a bell, like the ones at school. Whenever I heard the bell I knew I could see the horse.

On one occasion, whilst leaning out to get a better view, Omi saw me about to fall out of the window and managed to grab my foot in time. This reason for the phobia came out under hypnotism years later when trying to give up smoking.

Eventually I had to return to my family. It was decided that the best method to achieve this would be for Omi to put me on a plane from Düsseldorf to Croydon Airport (presumably the forerunner to Gatwick?) and hand me over to the crew and get off.

This is what happened. Unsurprisingly, I screamed the place down. To pacify me the stewardess took me to the Galley where the Steward was preparing food. This held my interest for a while, food always has, but the novelty wore off eventually. The First Officer apparently came out of the flight deck to see what all the noise was about. He took me to sit on his lap to pacify me. I can actually remember looking at clouds coming towards us and holding my arm in front of my face thinking we were about to crash into them.

Eventually (pre jet travel) we landed at Croydon. In those days you could walk up to an aircraft on the apron. My Mother saw the 'plane empty, and was becoming more and more concerned that she hadn't seen me. Had I missed the flight? Had Omi put me on the wrong aircraft?

The crew then exited the 'plane. The First Officer with me on his shoulders wearing his cap, with my pockets full of little salt and pepper containers.

Always ready to make a big entrance.

Apparently, that aircraft, but with a different crew was the one carrying Busbys Babes to the Munich Air Disaster!!!

Most of available holidays were spent in Germany with Omi and Opi. They took us on holiday to the South East of Germany to a farm.

As you can imagine, this was a dream come true to small boys. We rode on tractors and helped with livestock.

Opi LOVED mushrooms.

One day (I don't remember but I've been told it several times) we all went out mushroom hunting, Opi carrying a large old fashioned whicker basket to hold his treasures.

Apparently we walked miles but he had filled this large basket with a variety of different juicy fungi.

The farmer was astonished. He wanted to know where this treasure trove had been hiding. Opi offered to show him.

A while later, Opi returned with the farmer, both ashen faced.

The reason that the farmer wasn't aware of this place with all this bounty was, that we, as a family, had walked through a border mine field.

BOTH WAYS.

As a child you are often unaware just how close you came to not existing !!

So, my older brother, always the serious one, me always the opposite, was already at school in the village on the outskirts of London where we now lived, Roehampton. He, and later all of us, would attend Roehampton Church School. A 10 minute walk away, before the days when people drove their kids to school.

I, having been born in the June, started school in September as the youngest in the class of 5 year olds. I was 4 and 3 months. I remember it as being very intimidating. We each had a wooden desk with a lid that lifted to reveal the contents. We had ink wells that the teacher would refill, and dip pens, which were like tiny spears with the sharpened nibs. To write with them, you literally dipped them in the ink and wrote until the ink ran out then dipped again and so on. It was a messy business.

Most of our exercise books were covered in blotches of ink. I don't remember much about the lessons, other than being bored. So, from an early age I used to mess about and became the class clown. Often being told off and occasionally being hit on the hands several times with a bamboo cane. If you cried, as I inevitably did, as it bloody hurt, you got an extra whack. Such heroes those teachers. No doubt there were a few dubious wrong uns amongst them.

It was considered normal then so you just put up with it.

For some of my pre-school years I often had tonsillitis, and was, as a consequence, a slim child. It hurt to swallow. In those days, they routinely took you to surgery to remove your tonsils, as they subsequently did with mine.

I remember two things from it. My Mother had given me a toy corgi fire engine to play with to keep me happy. Apparently a nurse took it upon herself to "give" my fire engine to another child she thought more deserving. Thieving cow. The other thing was you got to eat loads of ice cream to soothe your throat after surgery.

Me aged about 4

CHAPTER 2

PRIMARY SCHOOL - SECONDARY SCHOOL

MY PRIMARY SCHOOL was a "Church" school. That doesn't mean that all we did was study the bible, but the governors of the school were controlled by the Church of England.

Other schools were Catholic, and, in the present day there are schools of Judaism, Islam and pretty much every kind you can think of.

I didn't at that age yet know that I would become an atheist who hates organised religion.

I don't hate the people who go to church etc, that's their freedom of choice, it's the Power-play behind all religions that I'm against.

More people have died in history through wars and conflict between rival teams of worship than any other reason.

It's about power and money.

Recent revelations have proved it to be evil regarding abuse, both sexually and emotionally in so many vile ways.

But, back when I was little, like most of us, I believed the lies. It was a Church school, attached physically and mentally to an actual church.

I joined the choir. Wore the fancy dress and sang the songs. As far as I am aware I wasn't personally abused by anyone other than my shit of a father so I got away with it.

I was regularly bullied for two reasons, firstly the obvious crime of my Mother being German. She, despite being 11 when WW2 started, had obviously been personally responsible for the Holocaust, and secondly l, because for a combination of the removal of my sore throats, and Omis Olympic training of calorie consumption, was a bit plump.

I had also already started to play the violin. Being both lazy and gifted, I could just listen to a piece of music and faithfully reproduce it by ear. My Mother was proud of me so organised private lessons with the school music teacher.

Mr Islewn (apologies if I've misspelled that) Lewis. A very fat bald Welshman who as part payment for these lessons would sit in our sitting room (that's maybe where its name came from) with a tray on his lap, munching away on a hot meal my Mother had prepared, as he barked out his instructions. He was one of the first people I ever knew to drive a Mini when they first came out. He must have had a very large shoehorn somewhere to allow him in and out of it.

He also thought I was gifted. Not just to keep him fed apparently. One day in the school "orchestra" (stretching the word in a big way) he gave us a new piece to play and asked me to start it.

The mass of lines and squiggles in front of me may as well have been hyrogliphics for all the sense they made to me. He was apoplectic when I told him I couldn't read music. Took it as a personal subterfuge on my part to embarrass him.

Off he stormed to inform my Mother, who had never assumed I COULD read sheet music. So, the solution was a scholarship to the London Academy of Music to learn it properly.

I eventually passed grade 8 by the time I was 10 (that's pretty smart if you're in the know). One thing really stood in the way of my continuing playing (well two if you include people continuously asking me if I had a machine gun in my case) was namely my aforementioned laziness.

Success with a musical instrument involves hours of practice. That wasn't on my agenda at all. I've always had a real talent for laziness. I've indulged myself in it's warm embrace in most things in my life, in particular in the avoidance of any physical exercise.

I continued attending the Saturday morning LAM lessons into secondary school but it was running out of steam in my list of things I could be lazy with.

So, I bumbled my way through school, mostly bored but I have a brain that could whip out a good performance for an exam. Unlike my older brother who resented my ability as he had to work his arse off to get good grades.

In those days in London, there was a life-deciding ordeal known as The Eleven Plus. Depending on your performance (at 10 and a quarter in my case) your future educational path was cast in stone for you.

Grammar school for the ones who turned in a good performance on the day, Secondary Modern for the rest.

A ludicrous example of how I don't believe schools provide much in the way of actual education for a life, but a way to get exam results that made the school look good.

Our amazing, always glamorous Mother

CHAPTER 3

SECONDARY SCHOOL

I WAS IN THE top 3 kids results in the London Area, so I was duly presented with a scholarship to a certain well known school in Westminster. I despised every minute of it. It was brutal. I was caned almost every day for the pleasure of some pervert on the flimsiest excuse.

Surprise surprise, those old two reasons for bullying me followed me there. I was a bit bored with it to be honest and, like many before me turned to humour and trying to be the class clown as a defence mechanism.

To add to my joyous attendance at the school, actually getting there was an ordeal. It involved a bus ride for about 5 miles followed by about 10 stops on the Tube (Londons underground railway system, the oldest in the World) followed by another bus. I was exhausted before I even got to the school.

We would have tedious lessons in such useful subjects like Latin, Algebra (what the hell is THAT useful for) and other wastes of my valuable time. Probably the only Subject I enjoyed was English. I've always found it easy to write.

Even the teachers were at it. The RE teacher was a weasel of a man who also carried out the compulsory swimming lessons. (Religion and watching boys change their clothes, a pattern forming here?)

To this day I haven't learned properly to swim, but this wasn't optional. To add insult to injury, it was after school in OUR own time.

Mr Weasel gave us homework in his objectionable subject, and then promptly marched us down to Westminster baths to the drowning initiation. Probably why I never wanted to learn looking back on it.

Having wasted an hour getting wet, I then still had the journey home so probably didn't get home until about 6.30pm.

Next day Mr Weasel demanded our homework. I explained (like addressing the village idiot) that, he was aware what time I would have got home, having personally delayed me from doing so, therefore, OBVIOUSLY I hadn't done the homework. He proceeded to leave the class holding me (there's that abuse thing again) by the ear and frogmarched me to the Headmaster for a caning.

Something snapped in me that day. The Headmaster listened to the squeaks from Mr Weasel and told me to bend over the desk (!) for a caning.

I was livid at the injustice of it.

I just said "No".

"What do you mean No boy?" He responded.

I explained (he hadn't been given this piece of evidence up to now) about the swimming, the journey and the lateness, assuming that he would now understand and see the sense of my refusal.

He offered my two alternatives.

Be "flogged" on the stage at assembly as an example.

Be sacked. (Expelled). I accepted option 2.

I turned and left his office. As I closed the door (it was about 3 inches thick with a key that you could use as a weapon) locked the door from my side, took the key and buried it in the flowerpot outside the office, and went home a bigger man.

CHAPTER 4

OUT OF THE FRYING PAN...

HAVING HAD THE audacity to "throw away" the wonderful opportunity to go to the Posh school from hell, my Mother reluctantly allowed me to attend the local Comprehensive Secondary Modern school. Eliot.

I was now 12. Entering a school where they had all already established their friends and enemies groups. With a uniform as a plump kid (I swear I'm not making this up) with a badge of an elephants head.

It wasn't initially so awful, but the jungle drums had revealed that my Mother was German etc (to be honest, maybe from me. I was and am proud of her) so it wasn't long before the bullying started again.

Added to that I was the new kid with the aforementioned plumpness going on. One particular thug, ironically with a German surname, was particularly brutal with his gang (bullies always hunt in packs). One afternoon on my way home they were waiting for me. I got a good going over with fists and boots. They half ripped off my ear and took the leather brief case my beloved Opi have given me, and threw it under a bus.

Someone must have rung 999 as I was brought home in a Police car.

I was off school for a few days but they didn't seem to be doing much about it.

I went back to school fearful for what was waiting for me. Sure enough at lunchtime they found me. Lots of pushing and shoving. Then I learned something. He punched me on the nose. I would strongly advise you never to do that. I completely lost it. I had him on the floor and using his ears as handles was smashing his head onto the concrete floor until a teacher pulled me off him.

I learned recently that he was knifed to death in prison later in life. Karma

For a change though, some of the lessons were actually quite interesting. Art, I enjoyed (look how THAT turned out), I'm still a wizard at pub quiz questions that involve geography, and English. My English teacher is about the only one I can remember by name. Mr Sabine. An inspirational before-his-time English and Drama teacher. I liked him and he seemed to see in me ways for me to show off in school plays which I took to like that duck with the water.

Like all boys I liked girls but had no idea how to deal with them. I was painfully shy and not the most attractive specimen available. I also hadn't learned to recognise what I thought of as a return of my advances as something less nice. A stunning girl called Cheryl Jackson arrived in my school from what was then Rhodesia, now Zimbabwe.

Blond and tanned I and most other boys fell instantly in lust. I followed her home one day so I knew where she lived.

From then on I would ride my bike near her house just in case she came out and saw her ideal boy on his bike.

To my delight one day she came out and spoke to me. I thought my heart would implode.

She actually asked me in. Could this be me really awake? Her very nice Mum made us some squash. And Cheryl asked if I liked music. I would have admitted to anything to please her. She said we should go to her room and listen to records. I was worried about standing up in case my excitement was obvious.

We listened to music for a while as I breathed her in. Oddly I thought, she asked me about my hair. What kind of regime did I have? I had no idea what she was talking about but just nodded inanely.

She said would I like her to sort my hair for me? That would mean she CARED, and would actually TOUCH me !

Obviously I immediately agreed. She led me to the bathroom and turned on the hand held shower as she directed me to put my head over the bath. This MUST be love. She wet my hair and actually touched me.

I was in heaven as she shampooed my hair and rinsed it off. She said it needed to be thicker and she would help me with that. Be still my beating heart. She dried it and started doing something I couldn't see.

It took a while but she was with me and touching my head so I didn't care. I never wanted it to end.

Eventually it ended. She removed whatever she had been doing to improve my hair so caringly and held a mirror to show me my freshly PERMED hair and started laughing.

I wanted to die as she showed me out the front door looking like a plump poodle.

I hadn't enough experience to recognise someone pretending to show signs of what my naive mind thought of as affection returned, when, in reality it was just her making fun of me. Whatever my Mother did to reverse the look wasn't really successful so I had to go to school looking like that to all the sniggers from her friends that she had told the story to. Cow

There must have been something in the water at Eliot as Dennis Waterman, Pierce Brosnan and a couple of other celebs went there. PB was a year younger than me so obviously learned a lot from watching my performances. Shame he never learned to sing though.

The only other one I remember by name was the PT (personal torture) nazi. John Taylor. A Welsh International Rugby player who was an evil bullying cockroach. He hated me for being useless at PT and made my life hell. I have no worries about him suing me for libel as it's all true. He would constantly pick on me as the plump kid. I dreaded his lessons, nasty piece of shit.

Mr Sabine was at the other end of the spectrum. I loved his lessons. I'd write stories out of my head. He cast me in two major drama productions, Noyes Fludde and The Apothacary.

In the Apothacary, I had, at age 14-15 (and never been NEAR a girl) to be "seduced" and even kissed (be still my beating heart) by not just the most exotic girl in the school, because she was Canadian, but also, I thought, the most goddess-like female I'd ever seen. Michelle Köhler. This was for me to make poison for her to be rid of her husband so she could be with her lover.

For rehearsals, oh dear I got that wrong, can we go again? I think I wore 3 pairs of pants I was so excited.

At the performance (nobody but Mr Sabine noticed) I was so nervous about the kiss on stage that I forgot the lines and ad libbed a lot of it. Inducing a few laughs from the audience that were not in the script.

A couple of years ago, by fluke, I got in touch with her again by phone. She is back in Canada and became a well known poet, so go you Mr Sabine.

I was forced to do French at this school. Bizarrely they refused for me to do German as I would have an advantage over the other kids !!

The teacher was a sour faced woman called Miss White. She'll be long dead so it doesn't matter. Like an idiot I did a caricature of her IN my French exercise book and got caught.

Once again off to the Headmaster. He called my Mother in at Miss Whites insistence. Apparently when the old hag had left the room he complimented my drawing to my Mother as a "good likeness"

About this time my sometimes there but mostly not father decided that we were getting big enough to defend our Mother, and it was time for him to leave permanently. I remember helping to carry his stuff out to his car. He said "Do you still love your Daddy" I replied "If you're really going, can I have your electric blanket?"

Never saw the bastard again.

In the last few years up to this point, our Mother had been getting "ill" with what we know know was Schizophrenia. She had some in-patient time in Tooting Bec (local Mental Hospital) and I learned years later suffered the barbarism that was ECT, Electro Convulsive "therapy" where they strap you down and push high voltage electricity through your brain. Poor thing.

So, for reasons that are a bit confused (I've heard two different stories as to why? at age 15 it was time for me to go out to Work.

CHAPTER 5

THE WORLD OF WORK

I N THOSE DAYS you could literally leave school on a Friday and start a job on the Monday. Which I did.

I had the choice of two jobs offered, both boring clerical jobs. I chose the one I did as it paid £520 a YEAR against the other ones mere £500.

I had never HEARD of such riches.

Ironically it was very close to my Westminster school, working in a skyscraper called Portland House for a cement company.

Oh the glamour of working on the 27th floor looking down on my empire. The job was boring but I knew no different. The people I worked with were nice. My immediate supervisor had that late 60s long hair and a Mexican moustache look and was apparently dating one of the girls in the office.

Another girl from a neighbouring department would often visit our hallowed office space for paperwork. She was a few years older but I was smitten (yes, she had a pulse).

She was very nice to me but more in the vein of an older sister. She would share my table in the staff canteen and I was pretty much in love, once again reading the signs incorrectly.

We were friends like this for what seems like ages and to my shame I can't remember her name.

One day I arrived at work for the girls in my office to be in tears. I wasn't used to this as I had 3 brothers so was unsure as to how to approach it.

I asked my supervisor.

My girl friend had been killed in a car crash over the weekend. I wanted to die too.

She had apparently been a passenger in a car, before the age of seatbelts, which had hit a tree at speed. She was thrown through the windscreen. The number one record at the time was Elton Johns "Your Song". It has always stuck in my brain as associating with that time.

I went to her funeral. The first funeral I had ever attended. I wished I hadn't. The coffin bizarrely had a glass lid. Despite the best efforts of the funeral people her broken beautiful face was there for all to see. I can STILL see it, over 50 years later.

In those days I was paid weekly in a brown envelope that you queued up for on a Friday. Even I could work out that my enormous salary should give me the dizzy heights of £10 a week to lavish myself with. So, proudly, I opened my first ever wage packet to a surprise. £8 13 shillings and 8 pence. WHAT scam was this? I asked what the mistake was, to be told, like the village idiot, the difference had been stolen by the Government under some scheme called "tax and insurance"!

I was beyond naive then.

My Mother worked close by so I got a lift both ways. As people did in those days, I gave her £5 a week from my wages. The rest funded my cigarettes that I thought grown ups needed to smoke, my subsidised lunches and the odd treat. Rather too large a portion disappeared into the aptly named one-armed-bandit in the canteen. It gave me an aversion to gambling that has stayed with me to this day.

I still had no carnal knowledge of a female (other than THAT kiss) and it was almost my 17th birthday. My Mother, ever caring, insisted I had a party. I didn't have anyone to invite. I had no friends really and work colleagues weren't overly interested.

Just up the road from us was a teacher training college that became Roehampton University eventually. Bless her, she somehow informed them that I had a party on.

A swarm of hungry students obliterated her carefully prepared cakes and sandwiches like locusts. They were all gone in a short time having consumed anything edible.

I'd have to find some friends.

I can still clearly remember Christmas that year. Unbeknown to me, everyone got an extra weeks wages as a bonus. I'd never SEEN so much money. And, in a pattern that I still live with today, I needed to spend it.

Almost all went on presents for my Grandparents who were there for Christmas and my Mother. The only one I remember was an electric Remington razor I bought for Opi. He cried when he opened it. (As I just did remembering it)

I have always had such pleasure in giving presents to people I love.

By this time I was almost 17, and had already sneakily driven my Mothers car in a car park in Richmond Park without her knowledge. It was time for proper lessons.

Miraculously, my Mother, who was probably the worst driver there had ever been, passed her driving test on the second attempt. Therefore, her driving instructor must be some kind of god. He'd do for me. I knew very little about different cars but I was a man child so felt I ought to.

My first lesson was the day after my 17th birthday.

His name was Tom. He was about 6'6" and quietly spoken. His car for my lessons was a Mk 1 Lotus Cortina. I thought all cars were like that, and it set the pattern for the need for speed for the rest of my life. The lessons were todays equivalent of £1.25.

On my second lesson (of 5 in total) he had me doing 70mph on the Kingston Bypass. On my third he made me drive around Hyde Park Corner. He believed in baptism by fire.

I passed first time. My world just expanded. Any excuse for me to drive my Mothers Vauxhall Victor (with leather seats and vinyl roof no less) I would grab it. 836 YPC was the registration. Oddly I've seen THAT car a couple of times where I used to live in Nuneaton, 120 miles north of my childhood home. Happy to say that it still looked immaculate.

I don't remember much of an eventful nature until later that year when, on the tube to work, I woke up on the floor covered in my own vomit. Other than the obviously mortifying embarrassment I was ok but needed to return home to change.

I got off the tube at Putney Bridge to get the 30, or 85 bus home when I realised I hadn't any money on me. My tube season ticket was prepaid.

There was a row of black cabs. I asked one of them if he would take me home and I'd get some money out of my Mothers "secret" stash. Bearing in mind that I stank and looked like a zombie, bless him, he took me home to Roehampton and said not to worry about the money. Black cab drivers are famous for kindness acts like this.

Obviously something was wrong with me.

The doctor was literally over the road so I washed and changed. As you could in those days, I walked in and the doctor saw me. He did a few preliminary tests and said he wanted me to go for more tests. I had ECGs EEGs and blood tests. They couldn't pin it down.

CHAPTER 6

BIG CHANGES

So, shortly after my 18th birthday I was booked into Queen Mary's Hospital, just up the road for a Lumbar Puncture. I had no idea what that involved or I might have refused.

Onto the ward on my due date. New pyjamas worn (I've always slept in the buff to this day) I awaited my procedure the following morning. There was a very pretty little nurse (my future would be full of them) who was funny and friendly and made me feel a million pounds. Maybe this wouldn't be so bad after all.

Even in those days I was a bit of a poser and told her I was a poet (as you do). She asked me to write her one, which I duly did (no pun intended as her name was Julie).

She spent more time than she should have with me and I must have had a rush of bravery. I actually heard myself asking her if she'd like to meet when I was released. To my unbounded joy she said yes.

I had my first girlfriend.

I wouldn't recommend a Lumbar Puncture. They make you curl up in the foetal position and drive a long very painful needle, that felt about the size of a scaffolding pole, into my spine to drain some spinal fluid to test.

It hurt.

I'm sure I cried (I'm good at that to this day) as, to my wonder, Julie was there holding my hand. The pain had been worth it.

They discharged me the next day. I asked Julie again in case I'd dreamed it all and she confirmed that she would love to.

A few days later, she arrived at my door. What did you DO on a date, I had no idea. As it turned out I was also her first boyfriend so it was a bit like a driving lesson from Stevie Wonder. Neither of us, both virgins, had a clue.

Well you have to start somewhere.

It felt so natural and so amazing to just kiss each other. Before we realised it, the clothes were on the floor and we were on my single bed. Naked with a woman for the first time. We explored each other, totally oblivious of the time (it was the early hours of the morning by now).

We had to take the next step. I knew where what had to go, after a fashion from seeing naughty magazines. What you did when you were in there I had no idea. Neither did Julie.

I can actually remember me saying "is this IT then?" To which with hindsight, her reply would have made me collapse with laughter if I'd known any different. "Maybe we should move about a bit?" She said.

And so, we both lost our Cherry together.

Ecstatically happy I asked her to marry me. And she said yes.

MARRIED LIFE

I know. I'd be thinking the same as you right now, but I didn't know if I'd GET another chance so had to grab THIS chance.

We eventually got dressed and decided to wake my Mother with this amazing news (it was about 4am).

Bless her she didn't really ask too many questions (who WOULD being woken to that bombshell?).

I walked Julie home to the Nurses hostel hardly touching the ground and gripping each other's hands like drowning people. Luckily she was on the ground floor and the window was open. I climbed in that window many times since.

My Mother eventually did get round the next day to asking some questions. Her view on life has always been, if her sons are happy she is happy.

So the wedding was booked. I visited her vile parents (they ran a nursing home near Box Hill in Surrey). Her Mother was the Matron. Austrian, curmudgeonly and an alcoholic, they took an instant dislike to me and we pretty much never saw them again. They didn't come to the wedding.

At this time Mother was finally getting a divorce from the pig and had decided that, as her sons were all growing up and starting their lives, maybe she'd be better off back in Germany. Best decision she ever made.

The day of my first marriage arrived. We'd both bought new outfits. My Mother had invited a friend she had met in Tooting Bec, an elderly Polish baroness of some sort. Hey ho, my Mother was paying so that was ok.

We lived on a hill. My Mother had parked her car facing down hill as it sometimes was reluctant to start.

Today, it was reluctant to start.

She, with the others, got in ready for me to push it to bump start it.

Remember when I told you that she was a rubbish driver? Well that day it included not turning the ignition on for the bump start to work. There we were at the bottom of the hill still not started, with my Mother asking me not to swear in that way with her friend in the car. I was sweaty and hot and worried we'd miss our own wedding.

We started to walk, frantically trying to thumb a lift. Thankfully, a curious motorist wondering about this odd collection of people stopped and offered assistance bless him. The 4 of us piled into his little Riley and got to the Registry office in time. He took us home too and stayed for sandwiches and cake. My Mother inherited her Mums baking talents.

So there we were. Married.

CHAPTER 7

OUT IN THE WORLD

I'D GOT A new job working in the Personnel Department of a Shipping Company. My duties were to assist in recruiting crews. This was done in the East End of London in the Seaman's Mission. It was vile.

The mostly Ethiopian and Somali crew had very un-English attitudes to hygiene, and, in particular, toilets. If I tell you that the cubicles were lined with coarse grain sand paper you might get an idea of what I mean.

Once at sea, if they were so inclined, in the office, I would deduct money from their "Allotment" to send regularly to their families. It was all quite mundane. My eccentric boss would go shopping once a year and buy 50-100 pairs of socks, all identical so he didn't need to match them.

My only moment of glory and glamour was to be travelling with him to Rotterdam to "pay off" a crew at the end of their voyage contract.

This was always in cash. So, in 1970, we travelled to Rotterdam, collected £40,000 in cash in a briefcase from the bank (a not inconsiderable sum even in those days). The plan was to meet the ship on the Pilots launch. Join the ship (they didn't describe HOW) pay the crew and return home. A nice little Jolly I thought.

Pilots launch tied up at the dock, boarded without incident. He then cast off to join the ship. Even in the massive harbour there it was a bit choppy. Assuming that "younger" meant more athletic (schoolboy error on his part), he gave ME the briefcase. This would involve JUMPING from the launch to a flimsy wooden platform and steps let down from the deck.

You're ahead of me aren't you?

On my third or fourth attempt, I successfully managed the jump.

The briefcase didn't do so well. The good news was, I was safe…

They were not amused. When we got home after somebody else managed correctly to do what I had failed at, after a very frosty return journey I was advised that I should basically sling my hook !

Julie and I rented a bedsit, furnished, in Sheen, the other side of Richmond Park. It was on the first floor of a house, and had no curtains. As there was a bus stop right outside with double decker busses, we became quite adept at dressing in a crouching position.

Like most bedsits in London in those days, they were a 6 month tenancy and soon we had to look for alternative accommodation. A friend knew of a room available in Clapham Junction, which we took. Sharing a house with strangers either works ok, or it's a disaster. Ours was the latter.

It quickly became apparent that two of the other rooms were occupied by drug dealers and I was concerned for my new wife. One particular thug had lunged at Julie in the corridor. To my surprise I knocked him out.

We couldn't afford to move again so I had a brainwave. I went to Clapham Police Station to ask for help.

Inspector Charlie McIllwrick was very kind and understanding. He explained that they would sort it out and not to worry.

A couple of days later mid evening there was a thunder of boots on the stairs and a gang of burley cops burst in. Charlie came in our room and said we should pretend they were searching our room too to allay any suspicions. It was all very exciting and they took three people away.

He came back in our room and explained what had happened. Thanked us for our cooperation and suggested that I might be interested in joining to Police as well.

CHAPTER 8

JOINING THE POLICE

I HAD NO JOB so it seemed fate that I should apply to the Police. It wasn't a quick process. Lots of references and background checks later I had my interview at New Scotland Yard.

Very intimidating. 4 serious men behind a desk with a thick file in front of them. Presumably about me. Senior serious man asked me all the confirm this-and- that questions. Then another asked straight faced if I'd ever been in trouble with the Police. Thinking he was being ironic I flippantly replied that I'd hardly be here if I had. No smiles.

Same man asked "what about 4th November 1956?" My head tried to calculate that. "What about it?" I asked, adding "I would have been 4 years old". Even my Mother had forgotten this. As a little lad, aged you've guessed it, at 4 years old, apparently some hooligan had lifted me up to put a firework in a post box.

Not only did a cop apparently haul me off home to remonstrate with my Mother about the first class villain she had produced, but the sad git had actually filed a report about it!!

I breezed through the rest and was eventually accepted. Initial training was a 16 week residential course at the Metropolitan Police Training School in Hendon in North London. The idea of not seeing my new wife for 16 weeks was only made palatable by having weekends off if you behaved yourself.

What a shock Hendon was. Think Army training films and you wouldn't be far wrong. Somebody was always screaming in your face from two inches away. You had to learn stuff like "bulling" your boots, ironing, making beds, the "proper way" to wash and shave etc. But, just like the Army it was designed to give your group a common enemy in the sergeant. It worked.

Sgt Anstis (Toby off the TVs dad apparently) was merciless. We were terrified of him. One poor sap, who I won't name here, just could NOT coordinate swinging the right arm with the correct leg in marching. So we hid him in the middle of us.

We learned all sorts of Police type stuff. And had to do my nemesis, physical training. I clearly remember one day where we had to do a 4 mile run. "Sod that" I thought. "I'm cleverer than they are".

I wasn't.

I popped onto the tube with a 10 shilling note tucked into my sock. Oh how smug I felt until I got off at Colindale station to find Sgt Anstis standing in full comedy "you're nicked sonny Jim" pose waiting at the ticket barrier.

He knew someone would try it, and he had a pretty good idea who that might be. Ultimate punishment. Not allowed home that weekend !!!

I was gutted. I'd like to say that it taught me a lesson but I'd be lying.

Lots more studying, being issued with uniform for the first time which was pretty cool and being taken to New Scotland Yard for fingerprinting and swearing in.

I was reaching the end of the 16 weeks. Every Friday Georgie Waghorn would rent a little FIAT and he, myself, Rocky Delling and another guy would pile in to teararse it home. These two were my closest mates. Georgie was older than most and had been in the Merchant Navy. He would regale us with fruity stories of his experiences. Rocky had only just qualified under the minimum height rules. But he had ENORMOUS clown-like feet. On parade they would stick out like a sore thumb. They were to come to my rescue soon.

Towards the end of training there were two ordeals you had to endure to "pass out". The first was gas training. They had old wooden huts in which desks had been randomly arranged like the obstacle course it was meant to be. You'd enter at one end, they would light some CS Gas tablets (no melodramatic grenades) you then had to take off your mask and get to the front to sign a register.

I don't know why they call it tear gas as it's like needles being stabbed in your chest as you vomit. The clever ones took shallow breaths and got out. The idiots (me) held their breath. They had designed it to be impossible to do on one breath, so I got to the front and gulped a lungful of this vile poison making it more severe.

In the afternoon we had to pass a swimming test, and jumping off a "bridge" to rescue some moron who had thrown themselves in the Thames. You may remember that swimming was not on my list of abilities. Heights were also, if you'll pardon the pun, up there with my fears and phobias.

Rocky and I had planned for me to "rescue" him where it would really be the other way round. Rocky, with his outboard motor feet was a swimmer and a half. That bit worked. Tick. Then we had to climb a 20 ft diving board to simulate the moron rescue. I was on my own here. It was in alphabetical order so I was first. There were 29 people in the pool and I was still standing there, frozen to the spot.

Dear Sgt Anstis advised me that the alternative to being assisted by his size 12 boot was to jump. I held my nose and stepped off. What seemed like 3 minutes later I landed in a seated position, shot about a gallon of pool water up my arse and knocked myself out. Your hero had to be rescued with the Moron.

But, I passed. The next step was finding out where my posting was. I was pleased with Kensington "BK"call sign. And was also allocated a massive flat at Wray House just off Kings Road in Chelsea. I was a Cop.

CHAPTER 9

BEING A COP

LOOKING BACK IS always clearer in most things than being in the moment. Here I was, married, in uniform as a respected person.

Ironic really, as I have always been a bit of a rebel who lives life by his own rules.

I enjoyed wearing the uniform and, I suppose, the power intrinsic to it but I've never been great at being told what to do.

Rewind to my first appearance at BK, a semi modern building in between Kensington proper and Earls Court.

PC106B (me) looking VERY young

Like many jobs they feel that you need to pass an initiation.

I had my images in my head about catching criminals and being a hero.

My first role in the Police was to be shown how to work an old "dolls eye" telephone switchboard. There were lots of cables. An incoming call would make a "dolls eye" (it's what they looked like) drop. I would then take one cable and plug it in, announcing "Kensington Police Station, how can I help?" They would reply, and, to the best of my knowledge (i.e. not much) I would take another cable and plug it into whom they wanted to speak to. This was a large wooden contraption, older than the building itself, that you had to walk around from the door into the room.

I got the hang of that. It wasn't rocket surgery. Unbeknown to me, a colleague crept into the room without my seeing him, and gave the back of the exchange a thump.

Every dolls eye dropped at once and I assumed nuclear war must have started, making spaghetti out of the cables.

They got me.

Everyone had a laugh and I thought that was me in the club. My sergeant put me on the public enquiry desk next.

He said that they had had a laugh at my expense but there was one cop who always wanted to take it further and to ignore him.

Forearmed, I waited for something important to happen, like someone bringing in an abandoned kitten or a bomb.

Eventually a man approached in a posh cops uniform. Aha, I thought, this will be the one he warned me about.

"Are you Ashcroft?" He asked. "Yes mate" I replied.

He looked a bit annoyed at that.

He informed me that there were a couple of dogs in the pound downstairs and that Battersea Dogs home were to collect them in the morning. I was to make sure they had water etc.

"They warned me about you" I replied to the REAL Chief Superintendent.

I got fined 2 days pay and had to get some string to exercise the dogs in my own time after my shift!!

Over the Nick was the Section House where single officers lived. As I was married I had our huge, mostly empty flat. Opposite the Nick was a jewellers. Coming on duty one night the alarm on the shop was ringing and the owners had gone on holiday. 3 or 4 nights coming to work it was still ringing.

Then, the next night it had stopped. I assumed the owners had returned. When I looked at the alarm box, it was a mangled mess. Having prevented the lads in the Section House from proper sleep, an anonymous individual had obtained a ladder and a lump hammer and beaten it to death until the ringing stopped.

When you are new, they assign what is euphemistically called a "parent PC". Mine was an experienced cop called Allan De'ath (pronounced De Ath). His main skill in his job was work avoidance. There were not enough radios to go round a whole shift, so he would hang back until they were all gone.

This way he was untraceable once we had left the "Nick". On night duty he had several bolt holes in hotels in the area where a friendly cup of tea was available. I wasn't learning much in the way of good policing.

One day the sergeant GAVE him a radio at parade so he couldn't avoid it. He promptly gave it to me. We went out towards Earls Court which was a 24/7 place and a bit rowdy. Weaving in and out of traffic was a drunken vagrant who was likely to be run over. Allan pulled him out of danger, sat him on the side of the pavement and said that I should use the radio to call a van to collect him.

This was my first go at using an actual radio and, to be fair, in my defence, I didn't really understand the etiquette and phraseology.

I pressed the send button and said "officer needs assistance outside Earls Court station"

How was I to know that meant "cop in danger?" All hell broke loose.

It was like Blackpool Illuminations with blue lights. Cars, motorbikes, cops running with truncheons drawn !!!

I wanted to pull the kerb over my head and die of embarrassment. All for a smelly tramp.

Oh well, life moves on.

Possibly to get me off the streets and out of harms way, shortly after this I was sent back to Hendon for a driving course and a firearms course.

The real reason was that we had Kensington Palace and tons of Embassies on our patch and both of these skills were regularly required.

I thought I was a great driver. I was wrong.

They are the best in the World at teaching you to do it properly and unteach everything you already know. I thought the skid pan training was the hardest skill to master, but giving a live running commentary on a high speed "pursuit" was much tougher.

I finished as a Class 2 driver which meant I could eventually drive the "area car" Bravo 2, the sexy fast blue light one.

In the meantime, the first Police car I drove DID have a blue light on the roof. A Morris Minor "panda" car. To add insult to injury, no two tone horns, but a BELL. A well ridden bicycle would get away from it, and you could hardly hear the bell INSIDE the car.

But in the interim, some deluded fool had decided that it was safe to give me a gun to wear to protect Kensington Palace.

That job was deathly boring. Especially at night. I would sit inside a thing about the size of a phone box and try to stay awake.

Police dogs are normally allocated to one cop, they live with them and form a formidable partnership. Known in the Job as Land Sharks due to their teeth.

In the Royal Parks, in which the Palace was, the Parks Police dogs would obey anyone in a uniform that they had been introduced to.

My regular (well not SO regular as you didn't get to be on duty there that often) was a chocolate Labrador called Dylan. He was a darling unless I gave him the command "speak", at which point he turned into a terrifying snarling thing.

Some genius had trained him to give you a little nip on the ankle if you fell asleep (fines 3 days pay!!).

I got nipped a lot.

They try to harden you up as a newbie. I was sent to a suicide on the railway in South London. Some poor sod had ended their life by train.

There were bits all down the line. We were given rubber gloves and told to bring anything we found to the sergeant, who had better rubber gloves and a rubber apron and wellies. At the time I remember being appalled that he was whistling the Hokey Cokey, but learned that most of the emergency services use black humour to handle bad things.

Other than two incidents of note the rest of my short time in uniform was a bit mundane.

The first one was stopping Princess Margaret for speeding. I was with a sergeant on nights when she flew past us. He knew the car. She stopped. He said that he would do the talking. We approached her car, the window went down to release a cloud of smoke. Her words were "don't you know who I am?" My sergeants reply is burned into my memory. "As far as I am aware madam you are an errant motorist" bless him.

Nothing happened.

The second was in the area car. We had to take part in collecting something medical (not sure if there were donated organs in those days?) from Brighton 53 miles away, and delivering it pretty sharpish to Great Ormond Street Childrens hospital.

This involved 3 cars, all Rover V8s, and 8 bikes.

The convoy would just boot it and the insane bike cops would leap frog stopping junctions for us and overtaking to the next one. We were rarely under 100mph so they were bordering on suicidal speeds. SO much respect for them. My adrenaline levels took about three days to return to normal.

Then, something happened.

I was on nights one night and had a pounding headache. It was quiet, so the sergeant told me unofficially to go home. I rode my little motorbike home and entered quietly so as not to wake Julie.

She wasn't on her own!! My brain switched off.

The man was getting out of OUR bed. My instinct was to hit him but something stopped me. I grabbed him and threw him out. Then threw him down the first flight of stairs.

I returned to the flat and threw his clothes out of the window. I actually don't remember much more after that.

The next day she was gone.

I was told that the Chief Superintendent (remember him?) wanted to see me. Gulp.

The person who was in our bed had made a claim of assault against me. The CS had seen him and told him two things. Firstly that he was caught in bed with a cops wife, and secondly, that an entire shift of cops would swear that I was still on duty as I hadn't officially been sent home. He then proceeded to rip me a new arsehole.

I was in shock. My whole world had crumbled.

I carried on zombie like, not really knowing what to do. One night I was on duty at the South African Embassy Residence at Hi Veld, I woke up in the flower bed. That blackout thing was back.

I was put on sick leave and sent to St Thomas's hospital (nicknamed the Coppers hospital for its proximity to New Scotland Yard) for tests etc.

Nothing conclusive was found but I put it down to shock and stress. Either way, my days as a cop were over.

CHAPTER 10

LIFE OUT OF UNIFORM

No JOB, NO wife, and shortly, as I had to give up my police flat, no home. My World was taking a kicking.

As I was being medically discharged I was "entitled" to have a return of my pension contributions. Like an idiot I took them. If I'd have left them in they would have been worth many times more.

I'd found a bedsit in North East London and used the pension money to buy a bigger motorbike.

I never heard from Julie again. I was told by a neighbour that she had moved in with this man AND HIS WIFE!!!

I got a job as a Store Detective in Selfridges Department store on Oxford St. I was in my early 20s now and feeling a bit rudderless in my life.

The job was pretty unexciting apart from at the end of the January sales. We found a cash till that nobody knew about. Lots of casual staff are employed for the sales and some enterprising tea leaf had set up their own. All the cheques were still in there but the cash was long gone. I had to admire their cheek.

I remembered one crazy incident where I convinced a young lady that we should try to have sex on a (slowly) moving motorbike. We fell off and she burned her bum on the exhaust pipe!

CHAPTER 11

RE-EVALUATING MY LIFE

I WAS LOOKING AT my life and thinking it was without any obvious direction and more than a bit mundane. Isn't that the same for everybody? I told myself.

I didn't want to be like everybody. What to do?

I sat down and wrote a list of the things I could do. It wasn't a long list.

Drive a car, speak German, make major mistakes in my life.

Now what?

To start somewhere, I phoned the German Embassy hoping for inspiration. A very nice lady there said there was a company in London called German Tourist Facilities GTF.

Me aged about 23

Try calling them, she said, they may have an idea.

Why not, I thought, so I called them. I spoke to a lovely lady called Ingrid. She was German, but, married to a Canadian, had lived in Canada for a long time, and actually spoke German with a Canadian accent.

She was fab and asked me to come and see her.

I instantly took to Ingrid.

She asked me a few questions, one of which was, did I have a passport? I did.

OK then, I was to be at Gatwick at 9am in 2 days with my passport and to look out for a man holding a GTF banner.

Wow, I wasn't expecting that response.

Excited I got the train to Gatwick Airport, and, being me, was very early.

I hung around looking for this man with a sign, and, eventually I saw him leading a group of people to the check in area. I approached him and was asked to wait 10 minutes for him to get the check in process sorted.

The last time I'd been in an airport was Croydon and I didn't remember that, so this was all very glamorous.

He came over and took me for a coffee.

They had been let down by one of their travel guides. My job (yes it already was a job) was to fly back to München in Bavaria, with the people I had seen checking in, meet someone there and fly back with another group.

Was this a dream? What if I was sick when flying? What, what, what?

He then gave me a little bombshell that, on the return journey with the new group, on the 'plane, I would need to give them a little welcome speech. GULP.

He gave me some index cards and a treasury tag and suggested what I should say.

I was bricking it.

I wrote down the two speeches I would need for a "thank you and goodbye" and for the new group "thank you and hello".

I put lines in between words where I thought I would need to breathe and bound them together with the treasury tag.

Had I bitten off more than I could chew?

He gave me a bag to put this in, along with a wodge of blank airline tickets and took me to security to get an "airside pass" to allow me access into the departure areas if needed.

Baptism of fire.

He showed me how to fill in a ticket, this one was for me for both flights, and off I went.

I had a large drink in the bar as I waited for my flight.

They used Dan Air, an early forerunner of the budget airlines we are so used to now. They flew 'planes called a Comet 4c, that had, how can I put this charitably?, been around a while.

To me though they were the sexiest thing I'd ever seen. And I, to my utter amazement was about to get on one and be paid for doing it.

We hadn't actually discussed how much this pay was, I was so excited I forget to ask.

I hadn't even told Selfridges that I was leaving.

The flight was called. I joined them all filing on board and looked for the seat I was in. My boarding pass, unusually, didn't have a seat number.

When I asked the stewardess, she asked if I was the GTF representative, then pointed out that all the seats had been sold !!

WHAT? Would I have to STAND all the way? I asked.

She realised I was new. She kindly explained that I would be on the "jump seat". These folded down for the cabin crew to sit on. You've probably seen them on flights you've been on.

Ok, that wasn't a problem, I thought.

She then informed me that because they had a full passenger manifest, they also had a full cabin crew so MY jump seat was on the flight deck (what you might think of as the cockpit).

I pinched myself.

Could this GET any better?

She showed me in to meet the Captain and First Officer. I would get to know this Captain very well over time. His name was Jeep (nobody ever used another name with him) Jackson. Like many Dan Air flight crew he was ex RAF and had the handlebar moustache to prove it. Everybody to Jeep was "old boy" or "old girl" I LOVED it.

The flight deck of a Comet 4c (many of the aircraft were also ex RAF) was a thing of wonder to me. The roof was quilted canvas to soak up the condensation and deaden the noise a bit.

My jump seat was behind No2 as Jeep referred to his First Officer. Some of the flights would also have a Flight Engineer, who's seat it was I was in. Because of the noise, I also had to wear a headset which allowed me to hear all the radio traffic and conversations. I was getting PAID for this?

Unless you ever get to experience what I was, you maybe wouldn't understand the level of excitement I had on my first (and every subsequent one) takeoff.

Sitting in the paid seats you miss a lot of the drama that I was seeing out of the windscreens and hearing in my head set.

To this day, on every flight I'm on, and there have been a LOT, I still quietly say V1 as the nose wheel leaves the ground, and ROTATE when the other wheels join in.

So, about 2 hours later we landed uneventfully at München in Southern Germany. All disembarked, including me.

I met my new colleague at check in and my adrenaline started to rise knowing I had to do my speech once in the air.

Another stiff drink.

Everyone was getting onboard. Again it was full. As the stewardess showed me into the Flight Deck there he was again. "Back so soon old boy? Didn't you like it there? " I was part of the team now.

So, my second takeoff. They never reduced in my level of wonder and delight. 20-30 minutes in after the cabin crew had done their bit it was my turn. GULP!!

Thankfully there was a curtain to close to hide the galley. The microphone was an old fashioned telephone with a trigger to speak.

I got my cards ready, written in my best German and started to talk. I hadn't expected laughter.

In my nervous state I was reading them the "thanks for coming and goodbye" speech !!!!!!

What to do?

What my life has always been.

Improvise.

I sheepishly poked my head out of the curtain, gave them a little wave and launched into the proper speech.

I got a round of applause.

I learned later that many of them though it was an act, and deliberate. I got away with it.

Because they all had to collect baggage and go through passports etc I flew through with my Airside Pass to meet Jörg in arrivals. Jörg Pavel was the guy I met that gave me all the stuff on the way out.

I now learned that I got paid £40 per flight (bigger then than it seems now) but the real money was made selling trips on the bus to the hotel. He gave me the brochure to learn, and the list of hotels and passengers (forever after known as Pax, which is what airlines call them)

I would receive 10% of all ticket sales for excursions.

I should, at the end of each day, work out the total sold, deduct the commission and my £80 (2 flights) and give the balance with the sheet detailing it to Jörg tomorrow.

SO much to learn.

Luckily, having grown up in London and been a cop there I knew it well. I'd never been to Windsor Castle or Stratford on Avon, so I'd have to wing that bit.

What he didn't tell me was that I would actually be DOING some of the tours I'd sold !!!

So, all the pax were through baggage and passports. We went round checking their names off our clipboards and allocating them a bus number. I got the hang of that quickly.

Then, MY bus were to follow me like sheep (you've all seen this happen) until I'd checked them off again on the bus. Inevitably there would be some who got it wrong and we'd have to sort it out, getting their bags off the wrong bus etc.

So, we were off.

About 50 people to welcome and sell tours to in the 90 minutes before the first hotel drop off. I took to this like a duck to water.

I learned later from my pax that they thought the way I spoke German, like a child, was a clever act. It had never occurred to me that it was the only way I knew. They also thought I WAS German, which was a big compliment.

Successfully sold tours, we started dropping them off at hotels that I would soon know like my home. I don't remember exactly how MUCH money was mine from that first day, but it was a LOT

I went home, my head spinning.

As unexpected bonus was soon to present itself. Many of the people going my job, both for GTF and many other companies, were attractive women. Often, whilst waiting for flights etc this new little club would meet together in a bar.

This looked promising.

The next bombshell was the following morning when I arrived at the office in Bayswater to hand in my takings etc. to be told at lunchtime the first of the London Sightseeing tours was happening. And I was the tour guide. As if that wasn't enough to take in, 2 hours after it finished, the evening pub tour ending in a Chinese restaurant in Soho was also allocated to me. Thankfully, to break me in gently, the pub tour was to be two of us, as I had no idea where they were.

I would get £25 for each of these plus (what turned out to be) quite a lot in tips. I was loving this. One thing I learned early when conducting a sightseeing tour, (especially the European ones that were to come) was that, as I was at the front of the bus, I would see whatever was coming before the pax, and, before the days of mobile phones and the internet, unless you did my tour twice you had no way of knowing whether I had made some of it up.

My first one went well I thought. I made more than my £25 fee in tips which I shared with the driver.

How hard could a pub tour be? I thought. Actually quite hard as it turned out. The pubs were chosen for being historic and picturesque, but also large, as turning up with 40-50 pax meant getting to the bar was a challenge. I would warn them about this beforehand, but it wasn't an issue with Germans. They were already experts at pushing in.

The buddy I had for my first Pub Tour was a very gay Swiss lad who was very funny. I have gathered many gay friends over the years and have often found this to be true.

The only pub I can remember all these years later was The Prospect of Whitby. A Tudor pub with a platform over the river Thames. It was beautiful and they lapped it up.

The tour went well, and we ended up at the MASSIVE Chinese restaurant for the set meal. It was my first ever Chinese meal and I enjoyed it. The evening was coming to a close, and a very attractive lady asked if we were all ending up in a disco afterwards. I announced it on the bus, if you'd like to go to a disco at the end, stay on the bus and you'll have to make your own way back. A handful, all single women agreed.

Our London trips were all either Monday to Friday, or Friday to Monday.

We dropped off my buddy and all the rest of the pax, gathered in the tips and the driver knew where to take the rest of us.

Bear in mind this was my second day on the job.

They all enjoyed the disco and mingled into the crowd. Apart from the one who had asked in the first place. Her name was Frauke, she was 12 years older than me, married but here on her own, a Dentist, and gorgeous. She stuck to me like Velcro.

I didn't go home that night.

What kind of paradise job had I fallen into? Bearing in mind that this was the early to mid 70s, in my first two days I'd made over £200. This was literally unbelievable.

I didn't work the next day, I was otherwise distracted.

And so it continued. Some weeks I could make £4-500 in cash. I was a bit like Stavros if you remember him? Wads of cash in my pocket.

Shortly after this I moved to a new basement flat, in Holland Park and had arranged to share it with one of the guides from another company. Her name, I promise, was Eva Kunter. She was very pretty but this was purely platonic to share the costs.

Boy had my life changed in a hurry.

I thoroughly enjoyed every day of my new job, the camaraderie, the travel, the variety and the "fringe benefits" as well as a big boost to my earnings.

For the first time in my life I was able to afford some new stuff. Eva and I blitzed Habitat for fancy house accessories. Our flat was looking pretty good. We led totally separate lives other than regularly meeting up at the airport and occasionally being in the flat at the same time.

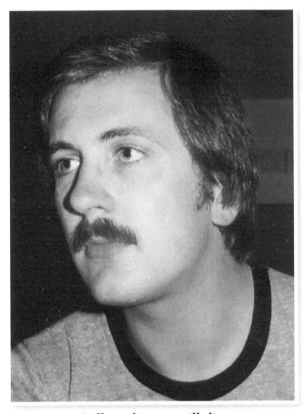

Still smoking so still slim

Frauke, the German dentist lady, managed to convince her husband that she needed 2 further trips fully to appreciate what London had to offer so I saw her quite a bit. Most people smoked then, as we both did, I find it amazing all these years later, when I've long since given up, how we could stand the taste.

So this was my pattern of my life for quite a while. I was in my element "performing" on my tours and was subsidising my brother Andy who was an art student, out of my princely earnings.

On a couple of occasions I even took ladies I was seeing to Paris for dinner and back the following day. It was only about 4-5 days earnings and I was loving the lifestyle. In the way that I pretty much always have done, blowing the lot.

CHAPTER 12

GOING INTERNATIONAL

AFTER SEVERAL MONTHS Ingrid asked me if I fancied taking on a European tour of 6 weeks for a group of American High School graduates, who'd been given this by their parents as a prize for graduating.

I almost bit her arm off.

A group of about 20 led by two formidable female teachers as chaperones, I was to hugely expand my countries count, meeting them in Rome. I went out 5 days earlier to check arrangements, meeting up with my friend Barbara who was studying art at the Academia Britannica. She showed me the city I was to fall in love with more than any other.

We also made that fatal mistake that friends often do and took our relationship to the next level. It was a shame because it ruined a good friendship, but was a lesson to learn.

I met some of our colleagues who were meeting a similar group and doing the tour we had planned in reverse. There would be a couple of occasions when our groups would be in the same place at the same time which we looked forward to.

For once I'd been doing my homework, making a thick folder that I still have, with details about our destinations. We went to Ciampino Airport to begin our adventure.

The first people I met were the two teachers Alice Honnell and Mrs Goodall. Both scary teachers who would take no nonsense from their group (or me as it turned out).

I'd worked out a system to keep track of them. I allocated each of them a number for the whole trip. As we boarded a bus, left a hotel etc, they would "sound off". If anyone was missing I would immediately know who it was, as would the rest of the group as we all gelled as a unit. I was only a few years older than the 18-19 year olds in the group.

The logistics of hotels, trips, and all the detail of the trip had been arranged by the travel company in Natchez Mississippi, in the US, where they came from.

The person making these arrangements had clearly never been out of the USA and plotted it on a map. Some of the distances and timings were impossible, and, in the days before mobile phones, left Manfred, my driver, and I having to make changes on the hoof.

I loved his bus. It was a very powerful almost double decker with air suspension and TWO toilets. He idolised it and slept in it at night to make sure it was secure. It was a Neoplan make, and light years ahead of what I was used to in England.

Manfred was a short plump man with a huge personality who knew EVERYTHING. Honestly, I couldn't have functioned without him. He had smuggled the woman who became his wife out of East Germany in the water tank of his beloved bus. He had Levi jeans and the newly developed pocket calculators to use as "currency" for our time behind the Iron Curtain which was VERY real still then.

We had two days in Rome with the group, then we were to fly to Athens for 3 days. I had never been to any of the places on the itinerary, so, if my research notes didn't cover it, I invented it with an air of authority.

Everyone fell in love with Rome. One member of the group fell in love with me.

I can remember our last night in Athens. I won't name her but, in the unlikely event of her reading this, she will know who she is.

We were in her room in bed. There was a pounding on the door. It was Alice Honnell in full Gestapo rôle. I panicked. I went out onto the balcony, 4 floors up. The next room was some of the males in the group. Their balcony was about 12-15 inches from the one I was on. I have always had a fear of heights as I already described, but I had a fear of Alice that surpassed it. I climbed onto their balcony and tapped on the window.

They let me in, in proper hero worship fashion. My street cred rocketed and I'd avoided the wrath of Alice.

The following morning we took our bus to Piraeus the port for Athens, to board a boat for a trip around the islands of Aegina, Poros and Hydra.

Everyone, including me fell in love with the Greek Islands.

The following morning we flew back to Rome to have Manfred meet us to drive the 3 hours to Florence. I've always had a soft spot for Florence, as I actually spent my 25th birthday that year on the Ponte Vecchio, fairly drunk.

They (and I) were soaking up the incredible history, architecture and scenery. From there is became a bit like that film If it's Tuesday it must be Belgium.

Next on our list was stunning Venice where we had an entire 24 hours to see it all. I've been several times since, we saw almost nothing really. One of my favourite parts of Venice is the island of Burano. Like an explosion in a paint factory it's brightly painted houses are truly unique.

You can tell that I still have that folder can't you? Remembering the itinerary almost a half century ago would have been beyond me. So, next stop after several hours in the bus was in the Alps at Cortina d'Ampezzo. Stunning mountain scenery and super clean air. Followed the next day via the incredible Brennerpass into Austria.

Quick trip to Innsbruck on the way to Mayrhofen (ironically where Julie was born. Remember her?) it was my birthday and I'd told them as a child how I'd worn the traditional lederhosen (leather trousers). They clubbed together to buy me the complete Bavarian outfit. It would have cost a small fortune. Bless them.

The following day blew their minds as we visited Neuschwanstein in Germany. Mad Ludwig's crazy castle. Think the castle in Disneys Magic Kingdom and you're almost exactly right.

On to München with the obligatory visit to the Hofbrauhaus. If you try to imagine the biggest pub you've ever been in, multiply by about 10. With the purest beers in the World.

Then back into Austria for Salzburg, Mozart and the Sound of Music (even if the SOM hadn't been filmed by then) they, and I were a bit blitzed by then. But good old Manfred then drove us to Vienna. We had 3 whole days here, visiting the Spanish Riding School and a concert in addition to all the incredible Imperial sights that beautiful city has to offer.

The adventure then became a bit more scary. For the first time for any of us, we were to go behind the Iron Curtain. It is hard to make you understand how intimidating that was, and some idiot had booked us into Prague on the 4th of July !!!

Many of us have visited what were the Soviet Bloc countries since the Wall came down but it was an oppressive scary place back then.

Literally snarling Border Guard dogs would be walked through our bus. At the best of times I find large dogs intimidating but these were particularly savage looking. Unsmiling Border Guards would take ages copying all the passports. In particular as we were either American or English (with the exception of Manfred). I was always guided by his advice. He'd been here many times and knew the ropes.

Prague itself was less colourful that it is now, maybe that's just my memory driving my outlook? In any event, letting 18 and 19 year olds loose on a city where their version of champagne (crimsekt) cost about a dollar a bottle was madness. Several got drunk and were dropping bottles from the hotel windows. It was ME who would carry the can if this went pear-shaped, so for once I wasn't their mate but in Alice's brigade giving out a bollocking.

The next morning we were to check out to drive to East Berlin.

The Manager said that a number of hotel towels were missing and he wanted payment in Deutschmarks.

I corralled the group and each swore blind that they hadn't taken any.

I was all for it to challenge the little shit but Manfred said that they always do this to get money. Also, if we left without paying his larceny money they would call the authorities and we would be stopped at the border.

I gritted my teeth and paid him. We crossed the Border into East Germany at a place called (I still have the stamp in an old passport) Hate. It seemed appropriate somehow.

Because Soviet Bloc currency had zero exchange value in the west, if you hadn't spent or disposed of it by the time you reached the Border, those vile guards would keep it. This explained why, for the last few KMs there were small children lining the sides of the road.

Manfred told us to throw it out of the bus windows to the kids. At least something good came out of it.

Manfred explained that we had a fixed amount of time allowed to reach the Border into West Berlin. Designed to prevent you picking up or hiding anyone en route.

We crossed into West Berlin through the ordeal that was then Checkpoint Charlie. Each person was roughly searched. Again with those vile dogs snarling. Many people were unaware that West Berlin was an island surrounded by East Germany. Getting in or out was meant to show the might and power of the USSR.

We had a tour of East and West Berlin. The contrast between the two was remarkable. The Wall was still very much there. People were dying trying to find a way to escape to the West.

I love Berlin now, it's a crazy city. In a way it was even more crazy then, as the surreal way of their day to day lives made it all a bit mental.

We were overnight in West Berlin before crossing back into what we genuinely felt of as freedom. West Germany.

Next stop was Köln (Cologne to the uninitiated) which was quite close to where my Mother and "baby" brother Mark lived. I called ahead for them to meet us in Köln. Mark was now almost 17. We all met up and the group adopted my Mother. I had an idea. If she could quickly drive him the 45 miles home and bring his passport, I'd sneak him onto the trip home.

Frantic driving occurred and Mark returned with his passport. Alice and her colleague were fine with our impromptu addition as we headed for Bruges then Paris.

He was welcomed into the Group. They all felt more like family to me now. The beauties of Bruges and Paris were absorbed and we headed for "home".

Manfred would sadly leave us at Calais and we would be collected in Dover by a new bus for the final stretch.

We sadly said our farewells to Manfred. The group had gathered a very generous trip to our little pal and we boarded the ferry.

The "luxury" coach awaiting is in Dover bore no resemblance to Manfreds motor.

We drove through leafy Kent to our hotel in London. For the first time in weeks I'd see my flat again.

The following day, I gave them my very best London sightseeing tour and they had the evening off.

Naturally, my inner circle were invited to party at my flat. Eva was away on tour. I awoke with a thick head not alone in my bed, but sharing again with the girl from Athens. It was an open secret anyway.

Later that day was a tour to Windsor Castle, probably the best preserved castle in the World. They were amused that we drove through Maidenhead (it had never occurred to me before) they lapped up the history as tomorrow was home time for them after the adventures we shared together.

I kept in contact with one of the boys, he would send me cassettes with music and stories of daily life. They were always entitled "Dear Limy, love Bacon" (his nickname). I still affectionately remember them as my first international tour.

Several similar tours followed but I was having more and more input into the planning. Eventually the company in the Mississippi suggested that it made sense for me to move there, do all the planning and just take them from there. Me living in the States. Wow.

CHAPTER 13

MOVING ON

WHEELS WERE SET in motion. My brother Andy was now living in Germany, and, as it cost me nothing with my bundle of flight tickets, I sent one to him to visit me. I waited at Gatwick for his very delayed flight. As I had my airside pass I would sometimes go into "the box" the bit above the check in desks and chat to the ground stewardesses.

That night there was an attractive Scottish girl on duty. She'd been on a long shift and I offered her a shoulder massage, as you do.

I sat on the desk with her back to me with her between my legs.

I must have been OK at it as she said she'd like some more. I gave her my address in London and she agreed on her next couple of days off to come and visit.

About 2 weeks later she arrived, with a case.

It was (oddly with what would transpire) a steamy affair and feelings were expressed on both sides. I had in the back of my mind my imminent move to the US.

I went with her to Glasgow. We stayed at her Parents tenement flat.

I immediately liked her Dad and immediately hated her Mother. She was a hard case in every sense.

Whilst there we went out one night to the Rolls Royce Club (her Dad worked there making jet engines).

In a moment of lunacy I asked her to marry me. I could only take a WIFE on my green card, not just a partner.

She said yes.

We had to sort the arrangements out quickly to arrange for her green card so we were married on the 10th of December 1977 in Kensington Registry office.

Fate was against it as the Travel company in the States went bust, thankfully BEFORE we went out there. I didn't want to be away on tours with a new wife so, sadly, gave that up. This meant I could no longer afford my flat and we moved to a cheaper one on Ealing West London. It was pleasant enough if a bit of a comedown.

I went back for a while to working in car rental. Her name by the way was Linda.

Shortly afterwards she had a miscarriage. We hadn't really taken any precautions. This hit both of us quite hard. I decided that day 21st February 1978 that if we were to have any other children I wanted to be alive to see them. That day, cold turkey, I gave up smoking.

Like most London rental flats they were 6 month leases so, soon, we needed to move again.

I found a flat over a carpet shop in Mare Street in Hackney in the East End of London. We seemed to be in a bit of a downward spiral. It had 54 stairs from the street !!

Shortly afterwards Lin was pregnant again. We went to all the parent classes and made friends with a young couple who were due about the same time.

Joyce and Andrew were Jehovahs Witnesses and lived nearby.

The women agreed (imagine this nowadays) that whoever went into labour first, the other would feed them ! Like we were incapable of feeding ourselves.

Lin went in first and I was invited to dinner with them. In their even smaller flat than ours, a roast chicken was on the table. Joyce suddenly put her head in her hands " are you ok?" I asked. She was praying. Oops Lin was to be induced the next morning so I got to St Bartholomew's hospital early. Even then, parking was impossible. So I left my old Fiat 124 Special (it was anything but) at the side of the road at 6am with a note on the windscreen explaining. Fully expecting for it not to be there when I came out. When I eventually returned to the car it was still there, no ticket, just a note from the traffic Warden saying "I hope you got your wishes. TW"

The Junior Doctor was called Dave Allen (I checked how many fingers he had, old joke) this was his very first delivery. They showed me into a room where they were doing stuff to Lin behind a screen. This is good service I thought as I devoured the toast and tea that was there. It was for her.

Weirdly from that day onwards, the only time I saw her naked was when our second daughter was born.

It was a year and a day after the miscarriage, and Joanne Felicity Ashcroft came into the World.

I think the one most relieved was Dave Allen.

I had a Parker Pen engraved with his and Joanne's name with the date. He was touched.

Believe me, trying to get a pram up 54 stairs isn't funny.

We settled into our little Family and, as is often the case, there was only time for the baby from Lin.

I accepted this as normal but like a lot of new Fathers I felt a bit like a gooseberry. The nice landlady bought us some flowers and I got talking to her about needing to find a better job now with an extra mouth to feed, were any jobs going ?

Her boyfriend worked for an insurance company, Sun Life of Canada. She said she'd ask him if there were any jobs going.

CHAPTER 14

BRANCHING OUT

OUR LANDLADY'S FRIEND came to see us in the flat. Unsurprisingly he said that, with a new baby, we should really have Life Assurance in case anything happened to us.

I sort of expected that. He said that there was a good career to be made in what we now call Financial Services. My main concern was that there was no salary. It was commission only, so, if I failed to sell any, I'd earn nothing.

That was a worry. I said I'd give it a try for a few weeks whilst still keeping my crappy job. I had to attend training at their office next to Trafalgar Square. With hindsight it was fairly basic stuff and directed towards you becoming an automaton to their script.

Early on I made a couple of sales to someone Lin knew. Lots of pats on the back in class but I really didn't know what I was doing. I didn't suit their "smile as you dial" awful script, where they would call a random number and you were handed the phone.

If it was me receiving that call I'd just put the phone down.

So I gradually whittled it down to the point where I was saying "hello, it's Mike Ashcroft from Sun Life. Would it be better for you to meet on Tuesday at 6? Or Thursday at 5?" It never ceased to amaze me that people would agree to a meeting with someone they'd never heard of and not a clue as to what it was about.

I would arrive at someone's house and basically say, I suppose you're wondering what it's about?

There was also pressure to fill your diary and scrutiny of your every move. As I've said before I don't respond well to that approach.

I also disagreed with their sales approach. It was all about selling them as much as possible and probably never seeing them again.

I have always been a relationship builder, and I looked at it as, I would sell them what they could afford, advising them that they actually needed more, so that was a reason to stay in touch and revisit the budget later.

Needless to say, the company disagreed.

I argued that I was building a stream of business that would continue to grow, instead of starting from scratch every month. I enjoyed the interaction with clients, many of whom became friends.

I would use a bit of simple psychology and, if I met a man who had £5000 of life cover, I'd cheekily say "you don't intend to be dead long then?" This was usually the first time that his wife had been made aware of the vulnerability.

So, I would ask the partner how she felt about it. If he went to comment, I'd say, "sorry, but you're dead. She has to figure out how to bring your family up on £5000".

I made a lot of men uncomfortable when they would get THAT look from their partner.

I would truthfully say that they needed more cover than they could currently afford, but, that putting this amount in place at least STARTED putting a safety net in place.

When I delivered the policy documents, I would ask them why they had taken the policy out. Then I'd get them to write that on the policy. That way, if anyone phoned to cancel, my first question would be, "what did you write on the policy?" Saving many cancellations.

I carried on with this for a couple of years whilst we moved to a maisonette in Walthamstow. It was nice having a bit more room and many less stairs. We muddled along being parents but the love and intimacy that I so needed was absent. She had taken after her Mother in her emotional disabilities.

At that time, every radio station was advertising "wonderful Milton Keynes" as a brand new purpose built city was needing to be populated. I lied to Lin as to how far it was or she would never have considered it.

We visited a swanky show house, where, pretty much, you chose a new home from a sort of menu. For the same as we were paying for the Walthamstow maisonette, we could have a brand new 2 bedroom house with a garden. It was a no-brainer and we chose a sort of Swiss Chalet house in Heelands.

The shopping centre was enough to make you move there, but the infrastructure for families was incredible. Schools, safe pedestrian walkways everywhere and a fast train to London from its futuristic main station. In no time we had moved to this wonderful place. It has its detractors and jokes about roundabouts and concrete cows but we loved it.

Soon the new neighbours were friends and all was good. Until the week before Christmas.

Baby clothes take a lot of washing and drying so we bought a tumble dryer. One night I smelled what I thought of as smoke. I'd put my car battery on to charge and assumed some battery acid has spilled on the carpet.

As I walked through the hallway I could immediately feel intense heat coming from the cupboard with the tumble dryer in it. The house was on fire. I screamed to Lin to get Joanne and her out as I rang 999 for the fire brigade.

One issue with a new city is, that there may be street signs where no road exists. The first fire engine was beached in mud. They called a backup which crashed on the way skidding on ice.

All this time I was trying to hold that door closed and could feel my back being burned through my dressing gown. I had to prevent it from breaking out into the house.

Lin, having left Joanne with the neighbours, came back in to help, and, in bare feet, stepped in a puddle of molten plastic that had seeped under the door. I yelled at her to put her foot in the toilet and keep flushing it. An ambulance and the third fire engine arrived simultaneously. A fireman dressed like an astronaut took the still burning tumble dryer and dumped it in the front garden for his colleagues to extinguish.

The ambulance was leaving with Lin with burns to the base of her foot. Mine were superficial so they left me there.

The lovely neighbours took Joanne and I in as the Fire Brigade wouldn't let us back because of smoke.

We finally got back in to our knackered home on Christmas Eve. Lin needed plastic surgery on her foot and we felt very sorry for ourselves.

I had pretty much had enough selling insurance and found a job in MK in an insurance company running the quotes dept. It was steady money and I liked the team I worked with.

Lins injury was healing well and we claimed against our insurance for the loss and damages. To my disgust they said that because it was mainly clothing that had been burned they would only pay 20% as it was "wear and tear". I explained that children grow out of their clothes so quickly they don't get a chance of W&T but they were not interested. Bastards.

About this time, somehow, bearing in mind Lins iceberg attitude to marital relations, she became pregnant again.

In August 1983 Gemma Lucy Ashcroft arrived to swell the family.

Lin was determined, despite the financial necessity of her working to bring enough in for the family, to be a (her words) "kept woman". She contributed nothing financially, but was expert in spending what I had brought in. She was Queen of the Catalogues, ordering ridiculous quantities of clothes. The girls often wore three sets of clothes in one day.

I pleaded with her to stop, and also, to at least get a part-time job to ease the financial burden. She was deaf to it all.

So here I was with a dead-weight wife who carried on throwing money away on catalogue purchases that we didn't need, at the same time as wanting nothing sexual and giving nothing emotionally. I don't half pick them.

About this time Maggie Thatcher allowed people to buy their council homes at discounted prices. I applied, and was surprised to be allowed to buy our little house for £17,995.

The mortgage was cheaper than the rent, which I was grateful for even if it made no sense. We slid slowly into debt with her lifestyle.

At work, the Regional Managers who were out on the road drumming up business from brokers, were on a good package in comparison to mine. Plus a company car. One of them left. I saw the chance to improve my prospects and applied for the vacancy. I got it. With about 30% increase in income and a car, a Ford Escort 1.4l in bright yellow. I was like a pig in poo I was so proud of myself.

I took to this quickly and enjoyed my new improved lifestyle. It didn't slow Lin down in her ridiculous spending.

My boss at work was head hunted to a new company Aetna Life, and asked if I'd move with him. I grabbed the chance. It was a new concept in investments and gave an exciting prospect for growth. I got a swanky new car, an Astra GTE with a digital dashboard. My area was anywhere north of London, and I racked up stupid mileages travelling around the country. I was basically in charge of my own diary which allowed me a new freedom.

I did 72,000 miles in my first year, usually at highly illegal speeds in my GTE. Initially operating out of our head office in Islington, but, in effect, working from home.

I was doing well. And was head hunted to Target Life. Even better money and car. Life looked good. We opened a Birmingham office. I was based out of there which was a commute of 85 miles each way. It was unsustainable. I started to look for a place closer to move house.

Most places near Birmingham were almost London prices with the loony house price growth that had happened in the 80s.

I spotted a sign for a new housing development on my travels, in Nuneaton. We went to see the show house and we're blown away. For the £49,995 that our MK 2 bedroom semi was worth, we could have a 4 bedroom detached with a big garden.

I grabbed it.

CHAPTER 15

NEW HOME, NEW COUNTY

MOVING TO NUNEATON achieved several things. Huge reduction in my mileage. Much larger stylish house with a garden 6 times bigger than our old home.

She still didn't have a job and the catalogue stuff kept arriving.

We moved the week after the 1987 hurricane and I was amazed that there was no damage for new fences etc.

I felt like we'd arrived with this new home. It was posh and looked like we were people of substance. I carried on with my mega mileage driving.

Target life were taken over by an old established company. Equity and Law. This was to cause a culture clash between the two sales teams. We were unconventional in our approach, had generally better cars and better Salaries. This was resented by the old team and caused some tension.

I went from basically working off my own bat to having to report to a man who just didn't get what we were about.

I started looking for a way out. I found it in an old South African company that was starting up in the UK.

I was back to silly mileages as my new office was in Cheltenham, once again about 80 miles from home. I was becoming disillusioned with the transient nature that my career was being taken. One of my Brokers I got on really well with, and started investigating jumping the fence to the Financial Advice side of the industry.

In the meantime there was a new female member of staff who was very flirty. We gelled straight away. She just came out with it and asked if I'd like to go to bed with her. As it turned out she was a bit of a nymphomaniac. I had nothing at home, so took the decision that if she was asking me to go to bed I'd be silly to turn her down. Very quickly we were having a wild sexual affair. I would leave my house, where Lin didn't give a damn about me, at 5-6am to drive to her house in Kidderminster for crazy sexual days together. She wore me out.

I didn't really feel remorse at home as I was in a frigid unloving relationship. This went on for several weeks until, in an unguarded moment, I was caught on the phone to my lover. As my daughters WERE important to me I agreed to end it.

I saw an advert in the local paper asking if you were under 40, wanted to make new friends, and, maybe liked a drink or two. It was for the Round Table.

This started one of the most rewarding and fun periods of my life. I joined and started getting involved in fund raising for local charities. Some of the best and silliest times I'd had were with my Round Table friends. In particular as Santa on their proper sleigh which we towed around at Christmas raising funds. I was (and still am) a natural. I loved it.

There were even trips abroad visiting other Round Tables with the same number as ours. I even took Lin on one of these. I think she'd forgotten how to have a good time.

At this time I made a major and brave decision.

Moving from a decent salary, expenses, nice car and pension, I decided it was time to jump the fence. I joined the Broker I'd referred to earlier.

No clients, no money, no car etc.

They initially helped me with some of that and I was now an Independent Financial Adviser.

It was a steep learning curve and I threw myself into it. Most of the clients they "gave me" (for a percentage of what I produced) were 30-50 miles away, which was why they were keen to offload them.

I persevered and started making a success of it.

About then, FINALLY, Lin succumbed to getting a part-time job.

Ironically allowing for her sparkling personality, as a Doctors receptionist. My Doctor.

She introduced me to him and his young wife to write some business for them. There was a spark between his wife and myself and, before we realised it, we were meeting to start an affair that would lead to her being my next wife.

Marriage breakups are always messy and painful. My marriage to Lin was ancient history. She just saw me as a cash source.

It was brought to a head when the Doctor husband, a small vindictive little man had lost his temper with her and thrown her down the stairs, breaking her leg. She had two gorgeous daughters, Holly and Lucy, who I'd got to know quite quickly.

They were almost 2 years old and 8 months.

She called me saying she was scared of him. I responded in the only way I knew how. I rented a house and moved us into it.

As you can imagine, all hell broke loose.

I tried to explain it to my own children but she had her hooks into them and they were fed with the one sided story that sadly often gets told.

I continued to pay her for the house, which she promptly used for herself letting the arrears on the Mortgage increase.

Things were changing.

Unbeknown to me I was being used. Samantha was having an affair with a Spanish Doctor before we met, all during our marriage and after our marriage ended she married him.

I won't call her names but she had 4 children by 3 different Fathers and was, and is, a fantasist and a fruit cake.

Newquay Close Nuneaton. On and off, my home for 33 years

CHAPTER 16

LIFE MOVES ON. ROUND TABLE

I'D BEEN APPROACHED to join Nuneaton Round table. Initially, my thoughts were that I preferred the company of women to a group of men. I've never really been blokey, possibly due to the fact that I'd never involved myself on organised sports (or disorganised if I'm honest).

Other than being in the Tug of War team at Hendon against the City Police, I'd managed to successfully avoid stuff like this. But, hey, it was worth a try.

Many people see RT as a lot of men behaving badly and drinking too much. There is an element of this, but they also organise events locally and nationally to raise huge amounts of money for worthy causes.

I quickly became involved in such fund raising myself. I was making local friends and contacts and was, for at least part of the time taking my mind off my personal situation.

We ran events to raise cash and had fortnightly dinners where decisions were made as to how to donate it and what social events were to be planned.

A highlight every year, on the closest weekend to April Fools day (April 1st) was High Tiddle. It had been going for years.

All of the Round Tables in the area would converge on a venue for a weekend of drinking. The object of the weekend was to climb a mountain, at least 2000 ft high and play tiddlywinks at the summit. Whoever won would organise next year. The tiddling would take place on the Saturday, in whatever weather.

Followed by a gala dinner with DJs and bow ties.

I attended such weekends 11 times, and, mostly due with being a tad under the weather due to Fridays drinking, actually managed to tiddle just 5 times.

I can remember one year, we were in Brecon in Wales. At the Gala dinner some bright spark had organised an Amazonian stripper to sell raffle tickets.

The chairman asked for silence in respect for the troops about to go into war under Operation Shock and Awe. She was standing next to me. I made an inappropriate comment about the Operation name sounding a bit like the ticket seller. It got a big laugh. And a glass of wine tipped over my head.

There were several international trips to visit other Round Tables with the same number as ours, 136. So I had fantastic times visiting France, Germany, Holland, Sweden and South Africa. Sometimes with partners.

Probably the highlight was in 1991. We entered a car in the Euroautochallenge. We borrowed the car from Peugeot in Coventry. It was a charity race (but each car was fitted with a tachograph, so the race couldn't include speeding) to touch each of the then 13 countries in the EU.

You could start and finish where you wanted but each country entered had to stamp your paperwork. 4 of us volunteered ourselves. It would take about 14 days including getting to the start and back from the finish.

We chose, because of the Bosnian Serbian war to start in Corfu (Greek) then ferry to Italy, then all the European countries followed by a ferry to England and ultimately to Dublin.

I could write a book just about this but I'll précis the story. The journey down to get the ferry to Corfu was uneventful apart from one of us (me) putting petrol in a diesel car. Swiftly fixed by Peugeot in France. Ferry to Corfu and back was uneventful. Then, using only old fashioned maps we did the other countries non stop. We all stank by the end of it.

We finished third in Dublin with 85.30 hours and knocked 9.5 hours off the World record.

WHEN would you ever DO something like that?

I ended my Tabling (they Chuck you out at 40) as President. I'm very proud of that.

Me as Santa in Round Table

CHAPTER 17

SURVIVING SAM

LET'S GO BACK to the start of Sam and I. I know now that I was being used, firstly as an escape plan from her husband (as he had MD after his name I called him the malignant dwarf) and ultimately to her Spanish lover.

Because she was a manipulative person, even he wasn't aware that he would quickly be replaced.

She was a District Nurse. Two things I am grateful to her for, my beautiful stepdaughters, Holly and Lucy, who still share a loving relationship with me in their twenties. The other was to introduce me to her friend Sue. Sue, and her now husband Gary are my oldest friends, there are no secrets there. We have regular gone on holiday together with our crazy group of what were their friends that are now also mine. I named us The Saga Louts.

We would usually go to a Greek island. It would need to be an all inclusive drinks package. We would then definitely not act our age. Often ending up fully clothed in the pool with more liquids in us than the pool held.

I "rescued" Sam and the girls when it was Hollys 2nd birthday the following day. Lucy was a baby. Sam was 19 years younger than me and, for a change, we had a good sex life. I had contacted an estate agent friend who had an empty house for a while. We moved in. Sam and I and the girls, plus (I wasn't expecting this) two large dogs.

When left alone in the garden they quickly turned it into a copy of the battle of the Somme. Even chewing off the step on the patio doors. I had never been, and had no intention of becoming, a pet person, but they came as a package.

Soon after I rented a 3 bedroom house in Exhall on the outskirts of Coventry. It had a huge garden and I thought would last us for ages.

I continued delivering money to my old home to pay the mortgage and look after my daughters. Unbeknownst to me then, Lin was spending it all and not paying the mortgage.

My beautiful Holly and Lucy

My own daughters Joanne and Gemma visited a few times and we all got on well. They loved Holly and Lucy.

We were planning our first holiday to Florida. Joanne was in the middle of her studies, but I suggested that Gemma would love it if she came with us. She'd get the whole Disney holiday thing. It was all sorted, she was on the booking.

Then, in yet more evidence of being a vindictive b**ch Lin told Gemma she couldn't go as we only wanted her there for baby sitting. She couldn't have told a bigger lie. So Gemma was deprived of what would have been the holiday of her life.

We were going anyway and I'd paid for Gemma. I suggested we took my Mother. Sam thought this was a great idea. I asked my Mother. She was still then a heavy smoker. She said she couldn't survive a 10 hour flight without a smoke. I said I'd speak to the airline, obviously a lie. I said they agreed she could have just one at the back of the 'plane. She knew I was lying, of course, but gave up smoking forever to come with us.

We arrived at our hotel on International Drive in Orlando, tired and ready for bed. The girls were sharing a single bed, we had a double and my Mother had one of those collapsible beds. I went to clean my teeth and heard hoots of laughter from the room. On investigation, my Mothers collapsible bed had collapsed. She was in it like a human sandwich, killing herself laughing, as Sam and I tried to pull her out (she wasn't thin shall we say?).

We had a wonderful holiday apart from what would become a pattern from Sam. She was lazy. She insisted every day that she needed a nap in the afternoon. This meant leaving whichever park we were in for her nap. She always said we'd go back for the fireworks. We never did.

When we returned home I saw correspondence from the mortgage company that, due to the large arrears, they were going to Court to repossess the house.

I eventually agreed a deal where I paid the Bond for her on a rented flat and carried on regularly delivering cash for the girls upkeep. She wanted cash so she could also claim benefits on top.

So, full circle, we moved back into Newquay Close with a huge extra debt to manage.

She had taken even all the lightbulbs, and poisoned my favourite Blue Spruce tree that I'd planted. The garden looked like a tiger sanctuary. It was (as she'd meant it to be) heartbreaking.

The divorces went through, we started planning wedding number three. Remember, all this time she was still having her long term affair behind my back, but still went ahead with the plans.

We asked our friends Gary and Sue to come with us and be our witnesses. We'd planned to be married in Florida.

Only a few weeks before, we'd attended their lovely wedding so it seemed appropriate. Sues two sons would come too, and, obviously, Holly and Lucy. We booked a large apartment on a golf course and started arranging the formal paperwork.

We shared a lovely holiday/honeymoon. We got married on the 11th green of the golf course, right outside the apartment. I wore a new Ralph Lauren (black) suit in 88 degrees f. I was soaked through in no time. Sam and the girls wore beautiful fairy like dresses.

We all went out for a slap up meal afterwards.

On a visit to Busch Gardens (a theme park outside of Orlando) we had temporary tattoos as a joke). I had a gekko on my right calf.

When home again, I liked this so much, as a little rebellious gesture just before my 50th birthday, I had it turned into a real tattoo.

Things were normal for a while. Sam told me she had dabbled in the past with sex with other women and wanted to try a threesome. Like most men I thought Christmas was arriving early.

Her chosen candidate was an attractive woman called Tina, who lived nearby. She had children and was a single parent. A plan was made to combine both families to have a short break at Disneyland Paris, and to include this threesome in the details.

I had bought a 7 seater Shogun 4x4 which was ideal. We drove there. Booked into one of those clean but basic French hotels with adjoining doors. The children were in one room and we were in the other.

Some wine was consumed followed by team kissing and touching. The girls were into each other and I was enjoying the excitement of it all, joining in where I could. I was sitting at the top of the bed, they were facing the other way, I was playing with both of them vaginally.

Tina said that she wanted sex as she'd already orgasmed twice, so I attempted to keep them both happy with penetration, one after the other. I'm no athlete but I was doing my best. Anyway, they'd reached the end of their own sexual journey that night and mine was about to end inside Tina.

Tina then returned to her room and I fell asleep thinking I was a lucky boy. I woke up to a frozen Sam. Ranting about how I'd been inside another woman. I pointed out that A. It was her idea, and B. She was there with me.

She was demonstrating her lack of mental normality properly for the first time and was telling me we were finished. The journey home was a tad frosty. I never saw Tina again.

Things deteriorated with Sam as she became more and more irrational. She said she was leaving and had found a house in Northampton, surprise surprise with a certain Spanish doctor.

I insisted on keeping my relationship with the girls which flourishes to this day.

I don't know what poison and lies Lin was feeding my own daughters but it was going down hill. They seemed to have so easily forgotten that I had loved them and worked my arse off to keep them in the ludicrous world of catalogues, whilst she had just milked me.

I carried on with sending birthday and Christmas cards and presents until one day the card was sent back ripped up in an envelope. The money wasn't ripped up with it. They cut me out of their lives and of their subsequent children, basically because I had left a frigid loveless relationship. Plus whatever fiction she had fed them. Eventually I accepted that they were gone and stopped sending cards etc.

My life felt like a mess.

There was the occasional female company but none of it felt right.

CHAPTER 18

ON MY OWN

WITH **SAM GONE** I had two ways of looking at my life. It was over. Or

It was beginning.

On TV at the time there was a travel program called "The Diceman".

It was a low budget show where a man filming it and the man being filmed would gad about the place.

They would go somewhere and film it, then ask random strangers to choose places for them to go based on the roll of a dice.

I don't know if it was rigged, but it appeared to be unpredictable.

I thought "I'm a free agent now, I don't need to ask anyone if I want to do something"

I needed a break. This seemed a novel way for me to choose the destination. I wrote 6 random places I hadn't been to and rolled the dice.

It landed on Reykjavik in Iceland. Two days later I was on a 'plane.

I landed at Keflavik airport to a bit of a culture and wallet shock. Reykjavik was mental. It was beautiful. It was brutally expensive. The people looked like Gods.

My ordinary (yet incredibly stylish and clean) hotel was a tad pricey.

I had 5 days to DO Iceland. I booked, as everybody does, the Golden Circle two day tour.

Waterfalls, geysirs, lunar landscapes and volcanoes. I asked the hotel for an iconic dinner venue. My plastic was as good as anybody else's plastic. They booked me a Billy-No-Mates table in the Pearl. A geodesic dome looking down on the city, and containing its own super steamed geysir.

It was stunning (as was the bill).

Bearing in mind that this was 2001, my menu was Sushi Minky whale, Breast of Puffin, and the most incredible lamb I've ever tasted.

There is no grass on the island so the sheep, eating nothing but herbs, come ready seasoned. I chose THE cheapest bottle of wine. My William (let's not belittle it by calling it the Bill) was £180 !!!

I walked into town marvelling at the incredibly beautiful people. Every shop or bar you went into, they gave you a shot of Brennjavin (?) their local aniseed schnapps. For free.

I loved it.

The next day I was picked up for my 2 day tourist special Golden Circle tour. Most people were in couples.

I was sat next to an absolute goddess. She was Italian but a lecturer at York University.

My eyes hurt looking at her.

We talked about all sorts. We got on well. I was beginning to believe in God.

We trekked around Power stations and waterfalls and canning factories and geysirs (which was how my trousers felt next to her). I was smitten. She was beyond beautiful, funny, intelligent.

And single.

She asked me if I liked jazz. I'd have admitted to liking tripe cooked in diesel. She suggested that we meet this evening at a jazz bar she knew in town.

Oh ok I said.

At my hotel I forensically showered. Wore my super sexy aftershave and cleaned my teeth at least twice.

The jazz place had a distinctive name so I couldn't go to the wrong place. My heart rate was like that of a frightened dormouse.

Obviously I was early. I sat at the bar where you could fill in a form for organ donation to pay for a beer and watched the door.

The music wasn't really to my taste as it was jazz violin. My £13 beer was lasting as long as I could make it.

The time had gone. Of COURSE she'd be late. She wanted to make herself particularly stunning just for me.

Even my ego eventually realised that she wasn't coming. Should I invest in another beer just in case?

The violin guy on the tiny stage asked if anyone would mind if a friend jammed with him.

I didn't really give a damn to be honest.

Then, stepping onto the stage was one Gordon Sumner (STING).

It was AMAZING so I summoned the strength to go for another beer.

On the tour the next day, she was very apologetic. Some family issue had stolen her evening. She didn't mention her love of jazz again, and I didn't tell her about Sting.

I stalked her for months until she took out a restraining order (of COURSE I didn't, I just thought I'd been a twat).

I adored Iceland.

If the price of a kidney peaks, I can't wait to go again.

In 5 days, with just a posh anorak to show for it, I'd blown £4000 !!!

Another milestone was being appointed as a Criminal Magistrate.

It took me three goes to get over the line. I felt that I wanted to give something back to my town. (Magistrates are unpaid, despite the fact that they have the power to fine or imprisonment. It's an ancient institution dating back 650 years where Justices of the Peace would rule an area and meter out justice as a lay person).

There was lots of training but no legal qualifications were needed.

I was sworn in at the ancient Warwick Assizes court. It was a circular court where defendants literally appeared in the "Well" of the Court.

I was invited to the Justices Mess Dinner at the Judges residence. It was a very boozy affair, the highlight of which was I got to sign the Justices Log that dated back over 600 years. How often do we get to do stuff like that?

Magistrates handle all criminal cases up to a level. Murder, Rape, Treason, Robbery would all be "sent" to the Crown Court in front of a Judge and Jury.

Magistrates dealt with all cases sitting as a panel of 3. The Chairman was the only one to do the talking.

After my initial training, I became a Chair of the Bench. I loved the variety of it, and the mix of people I sat with, and, even those appearing before me. Initially I sat in the old Nuneaton Magistrates Court whilst they built the new swanky Justice Centre.

I would sit 2 or 3 times a month, on everything from motoring offences to serious crime.

Magistrates are limited to imposing 6 months imprisonment or up to £5000 fines.

Only Judges are supposed to pass comment on a sentence but, as you can imagine, I wasn't having that.

I had many a stern look from the qualified legal advisers that sat with us to ensure the law was correctly applied.

I did 13 years as a Magistrate and had my 10 year Long Service medal awarded. I had to pay for it !!

Eventually I grew tired of the incompetence of the Crown Prosecution Service and very publicly resigned.

After I left I discovered that the people in the CustodySuite under the Court where sentenced prisoners are taken, called me "2 vans Mike" as the van to take people to prison only held 6, and, when I was on, they often had to order a second van.

CHAPTER 19
MORE FRESH STARTS

I THOUGHT MAYBE IF I joined a gym and toned myself up it might change. Plus it would take my mind off being alone.

There was a new one opening on the edge of town. I had never been to a gym before but they seemed friendly enough. I bought a few things to look the part.

I was a bit self conscious getting changed in a communal room but I got used to that. I signed up to a few easier classes. Easy is a relative thing. I found most of them quite hard.

There was one woman that I shared a few classes with that looked nice. I could never get to talk to her though as she was always with a Rottweiler of another woman.

I sat at the next table once in the coffee shop and overheard her saying that it was her 50th birthday soon and she was worried about a surprise party her family and friends might put on. She was dreading the idea of any male strippers or the like.

I had my chance. I asked my favourite receptionist about her. She told me her name was Diane but couldn't give me address or phone details for confidentiality reasons. She did know, however that she worked in the Hospital in the Diabetes Dept.

That was enough for me. I bought a card and a bottle of champagne. Wrote it as "Happy 42nd birthday", (every year I knocked 8 years off her age) and, that if she wanted to share it, my details, (with photo) were on my business card.

I took it to the Diabetes dept and waited for a reply. 5 long hours went by before my phone rang.

We arranged to go out to dinner, at what would become our favourite restaurant. I picked her up with a bunch of flowers.

We had a lovely dinner, it was all quite relaxed. I suggested that we didn't finish the evening there but take a drive to Stratford on Avon for a walk by the river (35 miles each way).

By then there was a charge between us. We held hands as we walked. After a while we stopped. A kiss felt right for both of us. Then some more.

We drove back to my house and for our first time went to bed. I took her home about 3 or 4 am and we arranged to call each other.

That had been lovely.

She called inviting me to her joint 50th Party with Chris Brown, who, coincidentally I already knew from our local pub quiz.

There were no strippers. There was however a huge surprise for her. Her Daughter (one of twins) was away travelling in Australia. Secretly she had flown back for the party and been hiding with a relative !!!

They announced that there were some flowers here for her. Out from behind a curtain stepped her daughter to absolute pandemonium!!

It was a lovely thing to watch.

We started seeing each other regularly. I'm not sure her kids approved of me. Bizarrely my own kids had been to school with hers. We lived about 200 yards from each other and we had both just come from a split relationship. With all those coincidences we had never met.

She was (is) 3 months older than me and a bit of a fitness fanatic. Even so we seemed to fit together.

One thing we shared a love of was travel. We were together for almost 18 years until we split up, and had 200 holidays. In fact only a few weeks after we met she came to a Round Table international in Germany. They were often themed these events. We all hired Tudor outfits. Obviously I was Henry the Eighth.

Nine months before my 50th birthday 9/11 happened in New York.

I'd wanted to go there for my 50th anyway and had been put in contact with the NY Fire department to take them a small tribute. They'd taken me in like a brother and promised to properly show me The Big Apple.

I hadn't met Di then so I told them there would be a change to my plans.

We were flying there with Virgin from Heathrow. When we got to check-in there were tv crews and balloons and bunting everywhere. Richard Branson was being interviewed. When we got to the front of the queue, I asked what it was all about. She told me it was their 25th birthday of Virgin Atlantic. Ever cheeky, I said that it was my 50th and could we have an upgrade. She made a phone call and we were bumped up to Upper Class, Virgins 1st Class. We sat at the proper bar on the 747 drinking free champagne. The food was amazing.

When we went to disembark, the stewardess give us a full bottle of Champagne to enjoy in NYC.

The hotel was central, opposite Pennsylvania station and not far to Times Square.

I'd arranged in advance for the Tourist Board to allocate us a Big Apple Greeter. These people give you a whole day of their time for free and even give you a subway pass in return for you buying them a meal.

Our BAG was an elderly Polish lady who walked our legs off showing us all around Greenwich Village and the gay fire station. She was amazing. The following day was my 50th and it was all planned out. First stop to the Lower Manhattan Fire House. They lost an entire shift of 17 men on 9/11.

The Captain who was about 7 ft tall welcomed us. I'd bought a case of beer to go with the small shield I'd had engraved.

We then had an emotional visit to Ground Zero. One of the saddest things I've ever seen. We had tickets off Broadway to see Les Mis so it was a full on day.

We did all the sights and took a helicopter flight around the city. I loved it. On check-in at JFK for our return, the queue for economy was biblical.

Despite Di trying to prevent me, I went to the Upper Class desk and presented our tickets to this very snooty check-in agent. He looked at it like it was dog poo and looking down his nose, reminded me that this was an economy ticket. He was a bit taken aback when I said "I know".

Like talking to a naughty child he pointed to the Economy queue. I explained what had happened on the flight from London and how Richard Branson had upgraded us personally.

I said how disappointed I was in RB as he said he would sort out our return flight too, and he'd obviously not bothered.

"Let me take another look" said Lord Snooty. "Oh here it is, I was looking at the wrong screen"

The Blagmeister did it again.

Shortly after, she convinced me to take our first cruise. I'd never fancied cruising. I'd been misguided. It was around the Caribbean. I was hooked.

The following year we had our first trip to Australia, with many other land and ocean based holidays, several with the Saga Louts.

In total I have been to 103 countries, many on multiple occasions.

CHAPTER 20

WORLD CRUISE

WE HAD MANY more cruises together, the pinnacle being a 14 week World Cruise, which had to be the holiday of a lifetime.

It almost didn't happen.

We had booked the cruise 2 whole years before the departure date. And paid in full the £5800 each that it cost. Working for myself, it took a lot of organising to take 4 months off work. Di only had one option as she was a senior nurse in the NHS. That was to retire. On her return she would then go back on a part time basis.

I told everyone and his dog that we were going on a World Cruise.

One of the attractions was that it was a small ship, only 400 pax. It was an old ship but they often have a bit more of a quirky character about them. Also, it was starting and finishing in England, which meant that the large volume of luggage wasn't the problem it would have been if it involved flying anywhere.

We were to leave on the 7th of January 2008, from Falmouth in Cornwall, one of the deepest ports in the World apparently.

On the 19th of December, just three weeks before we were to leave, the travel company, Travelscope, went bust !!!!!!

We had no idea if we would get our money back, and if we did, how long it would take. It was heartbreaking.

It was one of the worst Christmases I'd known.

Then, on Boxing Day (December 26th if you aren't British) ABTA, the Travel Regulator, announced that only ONE holiday from Travelscope was to go ahead as planned. OURS !

Van Gogh round the World cruise ship

We were going to have to sign paperwork saying that this absolved ABTA from further liability (happily). What we were not told, was that the Ship, which was owned by a different company, would only be paid on our return, to remove the risk of ABTA having to get us home if something went wrong. More of this later.

I had a 2 seater Porsche at the time so that wasn't much use to get us to Falmouth. Di had a convertible Mini Cooper, so, at least we could put the roof down, stack it full and raise the roof again. You couldn't have added a collapsible toothbrush to the luggage we crammed into that little car.

To remove any danger of traffic delays we travelled down the night before and stayed in a Travelodge nearby.

The big day arrived. We parked the car and they took all our luggage from us, we then got in the queue to sign paperwork and embark the ship.

The ship was called the Van Gogh.

Bearing in mind that there were only 400 people getting on board it went fairly quickly. Bizarrely, directly in front of us in the queue were two people from our town that Di knew.

We met two further people we knew. An ex colleague of mine that I met in the corridor, and the Dance Captain who used to dance with Di's daughter. So 1% of the passengers.

We got to our cabin (an inside cabin as it was thousands of pounds cheaper than an outside cabin. The ship was too old to have balconies) our luggage was there before us.

We all sighed a huge collective sigh of relief.

There was the obligatory lifeboat drill that all ships have to conduct, then we came to dinner, to meet the same group of people we would share every meal with for the next 4 months.

They all seemed nice enough. Soon it was grab a cocktail time for Sailaway. This is a tradition on every cruise at every port of call. Ours was even more exciting as we were waving goodbye to England for a LONG time.

I don't remember details about meals, but they were always good and we got to know the crew who would eventually become like family to all of us.

We were off out to visit the World.

First port of call was The Azores, a group of volcanic islands belonging to Portugal. The North Atlantic lived up to its fearsome reputation. I don't think Di surfaced from the cabin for several days. I luckily didn't suffer from sea sickness. As long as I could see the horizon I was fine.

Eventually we reached The Azores and found a chemist for Di. Next stop was The Caribbean, visiting several islands that we had been to before, but happily did so again.

One thing had bothered me. Di would happily spend 24/7 on a sunbed on deck. That had little interest to me. We tried Bridge Lessons from the wonderful Tony and Sheila, who became good friends. I couldn't get my head around it, and would be black and blue from being kicked by Di under the table.

What else could I do to keep me occupied on Sea Days? There was an Art Class.

I joined it.

Look where that ended up.

I took to this like I'd been doing it all my life. Brian, the teacher, was a darling. He was an old Cornishman. He wore a smock. He really did. He was travelling with his disabled wife. He had a wicked sense of humour.

These classes became popular and he had to add additional lessons. I fell in love with painting. A love I have to this day. I have painted over 500 pictures, won many awards, and even painted the cover of my first book.

Having cruised through the Caribbean and the Dutch Antilles, the next major excitement was to transit the Panama Canal.

The day before we were to visit the San Blas islands. Imagine a deserted Robinson Crusoe island and you've got it. As there was nothing there, the Ship would offload a complete galley and bars. A massive undertaking. We were told that normal service would be available and that we would meet a group of stateless nomadic Indians who would have stuff for us to buy.

It was impossibly beautiful. The Indians were all tiny. About 4 ft tall at the tallest. The women were in charge. They all had tattoos on their faces and wore brightly coloured sarongs. The hand woven goods were colourful and beautifully made. I bought two, one of which hangs still in my hallway, Di has the other one.

The food and drink was its usual excellence. A coconut fell just missing me. One of the male Indians produced an enormous machete and whipped the top off it for me. I took it to the beach bar where they added rum and pineapple. We shared the best Piña Collada I've ever had.

When we'd eaten enough the crew asked of it was ok for the Indians to have the rest. It was wonderful to watch them queue up and get food that they were totally unfamiliar with. I saw people with fruit, sausages, salad and fruit and ice cream all on the same plate.

It was also good to see a lot of the crew letting their hair down. They all worked so hard making it perfect for us.

Everything was returned to the ship.

We were to wake really early in the morning to watch us enter the Panama Canal. Truly one of the Wonders of the World.

We arrived early. The Canal is much longer and more impressive than you'd imagine. At the Gatun Lock at one end you are attached to a "Mule", a sort of train engine, that pulls you through the lock. As you can imagine with the size of the vessels transiting, it takes some time to empty and fill that volume of water, so it's all quite leisurely. We were in the next lock to a large cruise ship where the pax were making fun of our tiny ship. We shouted to them asking how long their cruise was. It was 10 days, they didn't even go all the way through the canal. We boastfully told them we were on a World Cruise to shut them up.

Even a small ship like ours pays $250,000 to transit the canal, such are the savings over going round the horn.

It was the hottest place I'd ever been. You could regularly see huge crocodiles sunning themselves on the banks. There were large raptors in the air. It took an entire day to reach the other end at the Panama opening to the Pacific Ocean. We sailed into the Pacific to our next landfall, Manta in Equador.

We had a full day here and were told not to go to Monteverdi, as it was "a hotbed of political unrest" so, of course we had to go there. We teamed up with the couple Di knew to hire a taxi. Pretty much it was just people in their own cars offering their services.

We agreed a deal with a man in a Suzuki Rav 4, not the largest of cars. Keith was about the same size as me, also an ex cop, so we squeezed into the car. We didn't see any unrest.

There was a fine cathedral and museum to see though.

We retired to a bar. I was curious about the curtained off cubicles. They turned out to be "cuddle booths" where private meetings could be held !

We split up for an hour and agreed to meet back at the bar.

I bought a proper Panama hat (they are made in Equador despite the name). It rolled up into a balsa wood box.

When we met up, Keith had bought a guitar and a CHAIR!! How we got all that back with us in that car baffles me. We stopped at the fish market to see massive tuna for sale for peanut prices, and langoustines the size of a babies arm.

We returned to our floating home having had a great day out. Next stop was 9 days sail into the Pacific to Nuka Hiva in the Marquesas Islands. Plenty of time to paint.

The Cruise Director decided we were to have a Pantomime to give our fellow circumnavigations near the end of the cruise, and was holding auditions in the theatre.

It was Dick Whittington and his Cat but quite tongue in cheek. I joined the auditions. The part I was going for was the Town Cryer (type casting?).

There was another pax about my size and age going for the same part. He went first and he wasn't bad. I'd have to raise my game. He sat next to me as I waited my turn. He must have been very confident as he started snoring.

I quickly realised that something was wrong. I shouted to the CD that we had an emergency and I with a couple of others got him into the recovery position on the floor.

If you're ever on a cruise and you hear "Attention, code Black" someone is in big trouble. The medical team arrived quickly with a defibrillator and started work on him. Someone said to find his wife. We scattered round the small ship with her description to get her to him.

We were too late. He had died.

We knew several people on other cruises that died. It's not uncommon. The problem was that we were two days sail out from Manta and seven to Nuka Hiva.

His poor new widow had to carry on as if nothing had happened for a week and go to meals etc.

The one bit of good news was, I got the part.

Eventually we reached the paradise island of Nuka Hiva. I'd been warned that there were very few excursion vehicles on this little island, so got on the earliest tender from the ship. I commandeered a long wheelbase land rover and held the sign to "sell" the spare seats for her. It was a beautiful island. We also walked for miles. I wouldn't put on any weight on this trip. I never used the lifts on the ship and we always got tons of steps in. We also did the "I walked around the World" daily mile around the deck for which I received ANOTHER t shirt.

I was keeping a daily journal and sorting each days photos to keep on top of it. It ended up as 152000 words and almost 18000 photos.

While we were having a lovely visit, the Captain had run into a problem. The Marquesas are French (there's your first problem straight away) and decided that Nuka Hiva wasn't equipped to take the deceased pax (don't people die there?) so, he had to stay in the fridge until we reached Tahiti in about two weeks.

Poor Mrs X. Still we didn't know so we were having a ball. We sailed down the Pacific visiting ever more stunning islands, including Bora Bora, Rangiroa, Moorea, and Tahiti as we sailed into Polynesia. It was paradise. And we still had WEEKS of this to look forward to.

In Moorea we took a boat trip in a small vessel to a place in a shallow lagoon where to could stand in shallow waters in a hatchery for sharks and rays. It sounded idyllic. As we approached the dock on this small island, I could tell something was wrong with the boat. We were approaching it far too fast as he desperately tried to engage reverse gear. He never did. We hit the wooden dock at speed and, riding up on it totally demolished it. He arranged to return after he'd dropped us to help rebuild it. We did the paddling thing and trepidatiously got back on the boat to return to the ship.

Halfway back the engine sputtered and died. We had run out of fuel with about a mile to go!!

We could see a French gendarmerie patrol boat speeding across the bay and were waving like madmen. They waved back and carried on. Eventually he did something and the engine lived long enough to get us back. He didn't get a tip!!!

The fellow pax we shared our meals with were lovely and varied. 3 couples and two single ladies. One of these was like a slightly older Joanna Lumley type.

Halette had sold her home in London and basically lived on cruise ships. Brilliant idea if you're alone and can afford it. It's certainly cheaper than a care home, with great scenery, better food and weather. I'm still in contact with her to this day.

The other single lady was about the only person on the ship that I wasn't keen on. She seemed to be a bit of a Walter Mitty and we never really gelled.

The poor deceased man and his widow left us at Tahiti. We later learned that this was the second husband of hers that had died on a cruise.

All these adventures kept piling up. After Polynesia next stop was Auckland New Zealand. I LOVE NZ and Oz. There isn't a single thing I'd change about them. Maybe apart from how far away they are.

Auckland is known as the City of sails due to the high level of boat ownership. Whilst we are on the topic of boats, the names confuse so many people.

These are the rules.

A ship is generally much larger than a boat. It has to be manned 24/7. A Boat is a smaller thing you often see hanging off the side of a ship.

Please do yourself a favour, and never call the cruise SHIP you're on, a BOAT.

Auckland was a delight. We walked MILES and went up the Skytower (1100ft tall) I even took a brave pill and momentarily stood on the glass floor.

There is a large road bridge across the harbour. It was running at full capacity and needed to expand. A clever Japanese company bolted another lane on each side to achieve this. The locals call it the Nippon Clippon.

We sailed to The Bay of Islands in North Island. This was a highlight for me as we were visiting a Mauri settlement. The tour guide was Mauri and explained the formality of it. We were meeting in the hall of their ancestors. Their Chief would "sing" (tell us) a story of their history. We would appoint a Chief to sing for us. They chose me. I was honoured. I had to sing about our Tribe. How could I do that? The guide had some suggestions.

We arrived at their beautiful settlement. There were carved and brightly painted totems everywhere. We would all approach the Hall of The Ancestors as a group. The Elders would approach us and decide if we came in peace. Naturally we came in peace. We all then received the traditional KiaOra welcome and rubbed noses. We all very respectfully filed inside what was quite a plain building inside.

Their Chief then sang about their story. It was truly moving. This wasn't some cheap tourism.

Then it was my turn to sing. I told them how we were a tribe that had joined together to learn more about the World. We were travelling on a big Canoe together. We were from many other countries tribes and were learning to tell our tribes at home about the world. I was genuinely moved by it all.

I lasted almost an hour. They then said that their ancestors would look on our Tribe as part of their own and wished us well on our journey.

What an experience.

On the way back to the ship we visited a Kauri forest. These incredible trees are similar to the Sequoia cedars in California. They could grow to 600 feet and grew almost 15 feet a year. They were often cut down by the Royal Navy as they totally straight nature made perfect masts.

Once back on the Van Gogh we headed the 1000 miles to Sydney. I've been there before, but NOTHING beats arriving by sea. We had float 'planes from the local TV station film is in from Manly Heads. There was a huge thrill as we approached the Harbour Bridge and the Opera House. We all cheered when the Captain sounded the ships horns as we went under the bridge (I'm not so sure that people climbing the bridge were so keen on it).

We docked in Darling Harbour. It felt special.

I have a soft spot for Sydney. It isn't the Capital city of Australia, but behaves as if it is. There is a spark and exuberance in everything she does.

I invested in three icons of Oz whilst there. A pair of R M Williams kangaroo skin Chelsea boots (which I have worn almost daily ever since as they are SO comfortable. In the same shop, an Aussie hat with a Coober Pedy opal in the rim. In The Rocks (the area around the city side of the bridge) an original aboriginal painting.

We were there for two nights so could explore a little further out. I'd watched a tv show with Michael Parkinson where he visited the most famous seafood restaurant just outside the city. Doyle's. This is my favourite kind of food so we got a water taxi to the bay which it proudly fronts. Walked inside and requested a table, to be told they were fully booked. I said that was such a shame, as my friend Michael had highly recommended it. They enquired who my friend was. Lying through my teeth I told them his last name was Parkinson, did they remember him? We got prime position table no 1. Di always hated my blagging something in this way but always enjoyed the benefits it brought.

So the next day we got the ferry to Manly. I much prefer Manly beach to the overhyped Bondi. Did some more shopping (how we were going to get home all this stuff I was accumulating hadn't yet occurred to me) and returned to the VG after a very nice dinner in Darling Harbour of delicious ostrich steak.

The last night we were there, Di's daughter had bought us tickets from the UK to see Billy Elliott. I absolutely loved it. The little Aussie kids giving amazing Geordie accents.

We were to sail away at night which was very romantic as we went under that iconic bridge again and out past the Opera house.

Next stop Tassie (Tasmania) about 4 days sailing away. If Oz is said (incorrectly these days) to be stepping back in time in comparison to the Northern Hemisphere, Tassie is like going back to the 50s.

Hobart is the obvious destination, but, as we seemed to be doing it on a budget, we docked in Devonport, which was asleep. We were taken to "an authentic aboriginal experience" where an obviously white guy called Kevin and his portly son were made up and danced for us. After getting over the wonder of that they took us to a really boring museum. The weather was deteriorating so the tour was thankfully cut short.

The Captain informed us that we would be sailing out into a typhoon that was on the Great Australian Bight (exactly where we were headed) and that it was "an arrestable offence" to go on deck. This was serious.

We started to exit the harbour and the wind caught the starboard side of the ship and pushed us aground on the beach !! They sent a diver down to check for damage which was just some paintwork, so we reversed off and tried again.

This had our attention by now.

We safely exited the harbour this time to the biggest waves I've ever experienced. Many people retired to their cabin. It was dinner time so I didn't. I was eating dinner literally looking UP a some waves!!

The old ship was made of tough stuff so on we sailed along the bottom of Australia, bound for Fremantle (for Perth).

3 days of slowly improving weather and in full sunshine we docked at "Freo" we discussed that we were the other side of the Planet and had one day here, followed by a nine day sail, through more bad weather to Mauritius.

It was crazy.

As was our decision.

We would leave the ship here, and rejoin her by 'plane in Mauritius.

We sorted it with the ship, caught the train to Perth (which I loved) found a travel agent, sorted the arrangements and headed back to pack some luggage.

Apparently we were not the only ones who'd had this idea as we found out later.

We found a weird AirBNB, dumped the luggage and went back to the waterfront area for an incredible meal.

We arranged a rental car and had a tour of Freo. Small but energetic would sum it up. We headed south in our car winging it towards Margaret River.

Everywhere in Oz is a long way.

We stopped at the recommended places, a very long pier, and the odd winery.

Stunning Whitehaven Beach in the Whitsunday Islands on the Great Barrier Reef

It was lovely scenery and totally different to the East Coast.

We found a nice B&B at Margaret River, a small town surrounded by world class vineyards. We visited a couple. They were a full experience in themselves. One, had a fabulous restaurant so we booked to return for dinner later.

Back at our B&B, I regaled the host with our day and told him we had booked this restaurant at the winery.

He asked how we were getting there. An odd question, I thought. Our car of course. "Oh no you're not" he answered.

We were unaware that no rental cars are insured to drive in the dark. Kangaroos. If you hit one it will spoil your day (and your car). So, disappointingly, we ate at an Italian over the road.

We'd travelled as far south as you could get to the lighthouse at Cape Leeuwin where the two oceans meet. We'd had a ball, but it was time to get back to Perth for our flight in a couple of days.

Back in Freeo we stayed in an eccentric pub called Rosie O'Gradys with full Irish dancing. The following day we gave back the car and headed for Perth Airport.

When we were waiting to check in a few others from VG were there too. We swapped stories. One man, an Englishman who used to be a colonel in the Australian Army was in with the right people and had us all upgraded to business class.

He asked where we were staying in Mauritius. I said it was a cheap AirBNB. He gave me a card with his number and said if it was no good to call him as his place was amazing.

It was a long flight made more bearable by the upgrade. We got a taxi to the place we had booked and Di burst into tears. It was the shittiest cockroach infested dump I'd ever seen.

They insisted we had to pay for that night but we had no intention of staying there. I called the number on the card our friend had given and he said he would send his driver to collect us.

About an hour later a friendly man in a Peugeot collected us. We arrived at what can only be described as a Palace. With a massive swimming pool on the edge of the ocean. Very tall ceilings, our room was the polar opposite to the dump we just escaped.

We met and thanked our friend. This place was run by an English woman with Mauritian ancestry. She was lovely. Her small boys pretty much lived in the pool. We were here for two nights before rejoining VG.

We said we would treat our friend to dinner. The hotel lady recommended a place for authentic local food on a posh scale. We all turned up driven by our loyal driver.

We were all really looking forward to our authentic meal. They had a "Special" that night.

Australian food !!

The following day, the driver took us on a tour of the island. To a Hindu festival that was just closing when we arrived. To the hills of the coloured sands, where dozens of poor giant tortoises were crammed into a space too small and too dry for them, where we were eaten alive by Mossies and a general drive around. My overall impression of Mauritius was, if you stayed on an all inclusive posh hotel on the coast (where, to be honest, you could be anywhere) you'd think it was paradise. If you weren't, I was very unimpressed.

The following day, we packed and got up early to see our beloved VG sail in. Just outside the pool area was a man washing and exercising a beautiful horse in the ocean.

We felt like we're were coming home re-embarking on the ship. Our little whim of a trip had cost us a fortune.

We greeted fellow pax like long lost relatives and got back into the rhythm of cruising.

Next port was the French island of La Reunion. It was a Sunday so hardly any taxis were about. We did a tour in the rain to see lots of waterfalls and ended back at the beach in the sun.

Zulu warrior

Next stop Durban in South Africa. I love South Africa, having been here a few times. I hated Durban. It felt unsafe, on every corner was a cop with a machine gun. We were to take a trip to Zululand in the Thousand Hills. That was beautiful and we enjoyed the Zulu village. I took a particularly good photo of a Zulu warrior which has since won me several photography awards.

Back onboard headed for one of my favourite places, Cape Town.

The waterfront and V&A area are electric and filled with exotic bars and restaurants. We took the open topped bus tour ending up at Table Mountain. The last time I was here was cloudy so it was nice to have full sun for the incredible views from the top.

We then caught the ferry to Robben Island where Nelson Mandela was imprisoned. We docked amongst the seals and walked to the prison. As you can imagine, it was grim. The stone quarry where they had hard labour, was a shock. The guide told us to close our eyes, take off our sunglasses and then open our eyes. It was like looking directly at the sun ! Small wonder that so many of them had damaged eyesight.

Back at the ship, we were told we had an extra 12 hours ashore. That NEVER happens. Unbeknown to us the ships owners were running out of money as ABTA would only pay them on our return. They were in Court in Cape Town over some money dispute.

We had all, in the Art classes put together an exhibition for the other pax. Brian had designed it and, bearing in mind most of us were beginners it went well. He also designed and we painted the set for the Pantomime.

After dinner, with everyone back on board, the Captain effectively "did a runner" as we headed out towards the South Atlantic. Obviously at the time, we were unaware of all this.

Psychologically we were on our way home now. The seemingly endless paradise we had been living in was returning to reality.

We had just 3 more ports of call before Falmouth.

The first was St Helena, the small island where Napoleon was held in exile. It was another place where time had stood still. The cars were British cars from the 50s and 60s. Known for two things. The place where Napoleon was exiled until his death, and the 1000 step staircase that leads up from the port.

The museum of the house he lived in showed uniforms etc that displayed how short he was. Naturally I bought the T Shirt.

We then went to the Governors house where, in the garden, we met the oldest living creature on Earth. A giant Tortoise called Jonathan. In 2008 he was 187 years old, so had been alive when Napoleon was on the island.

That night in rough seas we presented our Pantomime. It was hysterical and everyone thoroughly enjoyed it.

Next port was to be Ascension Island. We were prevented from landing due to the high surf. So, ever the rebel, the Captain said he would sail around the island to an internationally important bird sanctuary, Bosons Bird Island. Where, naughtily he would sound the ships horn to get the birds in flight for better photographs.

It worked. All us photographers had a banquet of bird photos, followed by a mega pod of about 3-400 dolphin. I have THE most incredible shots from that day.

The following day I "drove" the ship.

They turned off the auto pilot and I had to keep a needle on a moving line. I was rubbish at it as expected, and, after 6 minutes they turned the autopilot back on. The plotter was dead straight before and after me, and what looked like the plot of a major earthquake with me in charge.

We had a further two days sailing to arrive at our final port Funchal in Madeira arriving just after Dawn. I had been here a couple of times before and liked this little island.

Our cabin was an inside one with no windows. So, to see the weather etc, the tv was tuned to a Bridge cam.

We were woken by a very loud WHOOP WHOOP. Looking at the Tv, we were witnessing the VG being arrested at sea by a Portuguese warship.

We docked in Funchal with a ship full of rumours.

The money problems had caught up with us and the ship was under arrest. We, however we're free to get on and off as we wished.

To cut a long story short, the owners of the ship were arguing about unpaid bills in Court in Funchal. What should have been a 12 hours stop turned into 5 days.

We made national news back home with a GMTV tv crew interviewing pax at random. I received a text saying my PA had seen us on tv and what was going on.

After a couple of days (we didn't care how long it took, this was a bonus for us) the ship laid on coaches for a free sightseeing tour. We joked about getting back to the Port to find the VG sailed without us.

The rumours were growing.

On the fifth day the Cruise Director called us all to an emergency meeting. The bottom line was that we were going home tomorrow. The terrible news was that the entire crew no longer had a job or pay (or, in many cases, a home).

It was a very double edged sword.

That afternoon drinks on deck were free as they announced we were about to cast off for the last time.

We partied but there were many tears for the fate of our new family.

We sailed for home and started to pack the huge extra amount of stuff we (I) had accumulated. Keith and Pauline had driven to Falmouth in their camper van, they kindly agreed to take our excess back for us as they lived in the same town.

We docked in Falmouth. Lots of exchange of addresses, hugs and tears were had all round and we finally left VG for the final time.

Di's bar bill (she doesn't drink much other than Diet Coke) was £178. Mine was £3421

I hope I haven't bored you with the details of this epic adventure. I doubt I'll ever better it.

It took some time to readjust to being home and in that same routine again.

Off Ascension Island

CHAPTER 21

SPREADING OUR WINGS

SEVERAL MORE HOLIDAYS followed. We'd also been to Florida and noticed the value of the houses there.

We had a long discussion about it and decided to look into it on our return. I did the research and found a couple of UK based agents for Florida. One of them was only about 40 miles away so we arranged a meeting.

They seemed genuine enough and knew the market. They said that one of their Florida owners was looking to sell, would we be interested in looking at it. It was 3 miles from Disney World in Kissimmee just outside Orlando.

5 large bedrooms, 4 bathrooms, the master suite of which was bigger than my lounge, the shower could fit about 20 people and it had a jacuzzi.

The pool, like all Florida homes was covered by a large insect screen. It was a decent size, and best of all, it backed onto wilderness land that could never be built on.

Pipe dream we thought. Until we saw the price. £112,000 or the price of a tiny house in England. Without even seeing other than photos, we bought it.

2669 Autumn Creek Circle, Indian Creek was ours.

We'd better get ourselves out there to see if we'd made fools of ourselves.

Shortly after we flew to Sanford, about an hour north of Orlando, rented a Sebring convertible and made our way there with baited breath.

It was stunning. The quality of the furniture and everything in it far surpassed our expectations.

The plan was to use it as often as we could and rent it out in between.

We owned it for about 14 years and had many happy holidays (and many crappy tenants) in it.

Our gorgeous Florida home

When we were there and a hurricane was expected (they get a few there) we would throw all the pool furniture into the pool, as it's debris flying around that causes the damage. A byproduct benefit was that the chlorine in the pool cleaned the furniture a treat.

We had several great holidays there. And rented it out often. It funded our numerous holidays for years.

We eventually sold it to fund a large extension to our home in Nuneaton. Amazingly, the price hadn't grown much in all that time, but the exchange rate difference gave us a profit of about £40,000 which funded the work on our house.

CHAPTER 22

STILL CRUISING

TWO **CRUISES STICK** in my memory.

A Baltic cruise, and a Middle Eastern cruise.

The Baltic cruise ticked several boxes on my "not been there" list.

Sailing from Southampton it headed North to Norway. At the time I would have thought Norway was expensive, but I'd already been to Iceland.

Sunset over Venice as we cruised out

First port was Kristiansand. A pretty Nordic town that had the distinction of passing a submarine leaving the port as we entered.

Then we were to sail under the Orrefors bridge that joins Sweden to Denmark. It's a bit weird and I'd driven over it with Round table. It's weird because halfway over, it becomes a tunnel. Google it.

We were to sail under at low tide to ensure a safe clearance over the funnels. We were all on deck waiting to go under the bridge, when a Swedish airforce fighter overtook us below deck level, flew noisily under the bridge, and rocketed skywards in a spiral. It was better than sex !!

Next stop St Petersburg. I was SO wrong about St Petes. I expected grey concrete and severe buildings (it was my first visit to Russia).

What we got was stunning architecture (bearing in mind that it was FLATTENED in WW2) and canals. It blew me away.

From the Hermitage museum, that could take you a lifetime to see properly, to Catherine's palace, they all share one thing. Old fat miserable cows who want to bully you. I was VERY rude back. If they don't like it don't give it out.

The highlight for me was the Peterhof outside of St Petes. It transcended beauty inside and out. Topped off completely by the musical fountains.

Exquisite.

Next stop was one of my favourites. Tallinn in Estonia.

Think massive Harry Potter set and you're almost there. Stunning place. Give your soul a present and go there.

Then Stockholm. It was spoiled by the rain, but I will return one day in better weather. It's not just the 1000 islands on the way in or ABBA.

I was surprised by Gdansk. Partly by the silly cheap but rusting trains, to the square and that wooden crane thing. We had (me) an amazing Steak Tartare and a beer, (Di) a sandwich I think, and the ubiquitous Coke, all for less than €5.

It was a memorable cruise.

CHAPTER 23

ADVENTURE

WE WERE ALWAYS good at finding good holiday deals, but a 30 night cruise to the Middle East for £1300 caught our attention.

It was with a cruise line neither of had used before. Holland America. Sailing out of Southampton the lovely spacious cabin quickly felt like home. First port of call was one of my all time favourite cities. Lisbon.

I LOVE this place. From the quirky old trams to the fantastic food and drink, to the wonderful people. Before we arrived we'd already had our first medical emergency. We had to clear the upper decks to allow a rescue helicopter to take off a seriously ill pax. Apparently, he didn't make it. On shore we lost another who stepped in front of a tram.

If you've never been to Lisbon you're missing out. The world class custard tarts on their OWN are worth the trip.

Then onto Malta. I'd been many times but it's familiar. The biggest noticeable change was the lack of the old Ex-British brightly coloured busses. They were now the same as everywhere else. A retrograde step in my opinion.

On to Cyprus which always delivers. I never tire of Cyprus.

Across to Israel which was new to me. I'd started, as I often do, a pub quiz team. Two ladies who run a gay travel company, who are a hoot, an American lady travelling with her daughter and an elderly but witty Dutch couple.

We did well in our quizzes, winning smart enamel badges for my straw hat.

I clearly remember one quiz. The question was "who invented the CD Rom, which year and which company?"

It was HIM. The elderly Dutch guy. HE had invented it whilst working for Phillips. What are the chances of that?

He was in his 80s and had Parkinson's. He still had a wicked sense of humour. Next stop was Haifa in Israel followed by Jerusalem.

To my sadness I discovered that he had died of a stroke overnight. It was a privilege to meet them.

So, Jerusalem. On the weekend where the Muslim, Christian and Jewish faiths all had their important celebrations. The city was BRISTLING with army and police.

I loved walking around the history.

I was probably disrespectfully dressed in white shorts and an orange t shirt with one of my paintings on it, but, hey, I'm not religious.

We were around the wailing wall. We heard what sounded like gunfire followed by a large Bang.

Just outside the wall, above the Garden of Gethsemine a man with a rucksack on his back ran towards the gates. The gunfire was real, I don't know if it blew up his rucksack or, whether he did it, but that was the bang.

The following day we were on a trip to the Dead Sea. We watched a video of the above on someone's phone.

You cannot really grasp how deep you go into the Earth to get to the Dead Sea, but it's noticeable. The Sea itself I hated. It was very smelly and everyone just floated having selfies of them reading the paper.

I got some in my eyes and it bloody hurt. Never again.

Then something new. Alexandria in Egypt. WHAT a shithole. I'd pay good money to avoid that place again.

We later found out that we were the only cruise ship for 100s of miles and certainly the only one with an escort by a Royal Navy Warship. We couldn't see it but it was there. We were to transit the Suez Canal (boring in comparison to the Panama) and head out around the Horn of Africa into Pirate Alley heading for Arabia.

The transit of the Suez Canal was uneventful (boring) and we had two stops to look forward to in Oman. Another new country.

The first, Salalah, was nothing special. Just a mosque with an old town attached.

Muscat, the capital, however was a world of difference. Beautiful and incredibly opulent, the Sultans Palace make Buckingham Palace look like a shack.

At this stage of the cruise things started getting serious. We had Pirate drills with high pressure hoses, Decibel Cannons that would aim a beam of debilitating noise, and, ultimately, Gurkhas with machine guns.

From here on in, the rule was, if you hear the attack alarm, it's REAL. Go to your cabin, lock the door and stay away from the windows.

Exciting stuff. Nothing happened.

Then one day I was in a lecture downstairs when the Attack Alarm went off. Far from everyone going to their Cabin everyone went on deck to see what was going on.

Di videoed it.

Three fast ribs with machine guns came from Iran. They were circling the massive ship. They were apparently Iranian Millitia. Unbeknown to us the Captain had sent an SOS to the Royal Navy Warship. It launched its helicopter gunship. One sniff of that baby and the boats pissed off back to Iran as the gunship went flying past us in pursuit.

I bloody LOVE my life.

No more dramas. Next stop Abu Dhabi. Which I much prefer to Dubai.

We had a British comedian onboard. The multinational pax list didn't really get him. We did.

He warned us that Dubai don't like The Flintstones cartoon. Something to do with them being shown in bed.

He repeated it.

Dubai don't like the Flintstones. Abu Dhabi do.

We fell about. It was so bad it was brilliant. All the non Brits looked bemused.

One of the most beautiful things I've ever seen was the Grand Mosque in Abu Dhabi. It cost BILLIONS of $. The inlaid Marble artwork was exquisite. It had 4 three ton Swarovski crystal chandeliers and the biggest single carpet ever made. Big enough for 8000 to pray at once.

The taxi driver lent Di a full Burkha as that's what she needed. I was in T-shirt and shorts. I made the mistake of putting my arm round her shoulder for a selfie. Whistles blew. I was a a very naughty boy and was made to feel such.

We took a taxi to the biggest hotel in town. They genuinely have dispensing machines for gold bars. In case you left yours at home.

Next and final stop. Dubai.

Been there before but hadn't ventured up the Burg Khalifa, the tallest building in the World. Dubai is incredible. I'm there again in November. It expands faster than you can blink.

The Burg is over a kilometre high. The 180 floors in the lift is so fast you cannot actually feel it move. It starts relatively slowly then goes ballistic until the last few floors when it slows again. Bottom to top in about 30 seconds. The VIEWS !!!

FINALE

DI'S TWINS HAD 4 children between them and I adored them. Of course there were times when they, like all kids can be irritating, but I would have died for them.

Walking with lions in Senegal. Sometimes you just need to feel the fear and do it anyway

My relationship with Di had become Platonic. We rarely had any sexual life together. It wasn't her fault, there was something inside her that didn't work for me any more.

Outwardly we had everything. Lovely home. Great lifestyle. Holidays, friends. For me however, it wasn't enough. I needed full-on love.

We tried again and again but it wasn't fixable.

I was getting to the point where I was genuinely not happy in our relationship.

She was and is a very special person. She cares deeply for her family her friends and her patients.

Unfortunately she wasn't able to care for me in the way that I needed.

I am a very romantic and demonstrative person. I need to love and be loved in return.

We had spoken about it on several occasions. I don't think Di was able to change and I felt I had reached a point where I wanted to look for what I needed elsewhere.

There were lots of tears and heartbreak. We agreed that we would go our separate ways. Di bought my share of the house and I looked for somewhere to make a new start.

It wasn't actually friendly but we were being civil about it for which I was grateful.

Anyone that knew me said I was crazy, but it wasn't their life, it was mine.

Me in my beloved Spitfire

I felt that moving to a new town would be sensible. I found a lovely small new house 25 miles away and bought into it.

Split ups are always agony but I felt we'd done it with a little pain as was possible.

Tragically, her children decided that they would put their own feelings before those of their beautiful children and cut off any contact I had with them.

I feel that this is as cruel on the children who don't get a vote, as it was obviously meant to be for me.

I cannot influence their decision.

So, in summary, I'm living proof that you CAN teach an old dog new tricks.

My amazing life opens another exciting chapter amidst the biggest pandemic in living memory.

Carpe Dium. SEIZE the day.

Photo of Andy

P.S. This photo is of my brother Andy who died aged 57. A talented artist and sculptor his demons were too great for him.

Lightning Source UK Ltd.
Milton Keynes UK
UKHW050936101122
411941UK00002B/67